CHEMISTRY
for AQA

Ann and Patrick Fullick

Heinemann

Heinemann Educational Publishers
Halley Court, Jordan Hill, Oxford, OX2 8EJ
Part of Harcourt Education

Heinemann is a registered trademark of
Harcourt Education Limited

© Ann and Patrick Fullick, 2001

First published 2001

ISBN 0 435 58390 5
05 04 03
10 9 8 7 6 5 4 3 2

Edited by Linda Moore

Designed, typeset and illustrated by Gecko Ltd

Illustrated by Martin Fish, Paul McCaffry and Geoff Ward

Printed and bound in Italy by Printer Trento S.r.l.

Acknowledgements
The authors and publishers would like to thank the
following for permission to use photographs:

2: TR SPL/NASA/GSFC, ML SPL/Klaus Guldbrandsen,
M Andrew Lambert, BR Robert Harding; 4: SPL/Philippe
Plailly; 5: TR SPL, M Mary Evans; 7: SPL; 8: SPL/Michael
Gilbert; 10: Ace Photo Library; 12: TR Stock Market,
M Andrew Lambert, B SPL; 13: Andrew Lambert; 14:
Andrew Lambert; 15: SPL/Charles D Winters; 16: Robert
Harding; 18: SPL/Charles D. Winters; 19: Robert
Harding; 22: TR SPL/Sheila Terry, four pictures at bottom
Andrew Lambert; 24: Andrew Lambert; 26: TR Andrew
Lambert, B Corbis; 27: TL Andrew Lambert, TM Andrew
Lambert, TR Andrew Lambert, ML Andrew Lambert, M
Andrew Lambert, MR Andrew Lambert, BR Roger Scruton;
29: SPL/Colin Cuthbert; 30: GSF; 31: Robert Harding;
32: TR Andrew Lambert, BR Andrew Lambert, MR Andrew
Lambert, BL Peter Gould; 33: Ace Photos; 34: SPL; 35:
Andrew Lambert; 38: Robert Harding; 39: Environmental
Images; 41: Popperfoto; 42: SPL/David Halpern; 43:
SPL/Y.Hamel, Publiphoto Diffusion; 44: TR Corbis,
MR Roger Scruton; 45: Ace Photos; 46: Environmental
Images; 48: TR SPL/Francoise Sauze, BR Collections; 49:
TL Advertising Archives, TR Topham Picturepoint; 52:
TR Colorific, BR AA & A, BL SPL/Maximilian Stock Ltd;
53: AA & A; 54: TR Peter Gould, MR Andrew Lambert,
BR Andrew Lambert; 57: SPL/Maximilian Stock Ltd; 58:
SPL; 60: Corbis; 61: TR SPL/Rosenfield Images Ltd,
ML Robert Harding; 62: Ace Photos; 64: TR Ace Photos,
MR Ace Photos, BL Collections; 65: Robert Harding; 66:
OSF; 68: BASF; 69: TR Environmental Images, M Robert
Harding, MR Robert Harding; 72: TR OSF, BL SPL; 73:
TR SPL, MR SPL; 74: GSF; 75: SPL; 76: Robert Harding;
78: M SPL, B GSF, TM SPL; 79: BL GSF, M GSF; 82: TR SPL,
M GSF, B GSF; 83: TR SPL, M SPL; 86: TR SPL, BR Royal
Society of Chemistry; 87: M SPL, TR G. T. Woods; 89:
TR Andrew Lambert, MR Andrew Lambert; 90: M Roger
Scruton, MR Andrew Lambert; 92: BL Peter Gould, three
pictures at bottom right Andrew Lambert; 93: Peter
Gould; 94: MR Andrew Lambert, M SPL; 96: MR Peter
Gould, B Andrew Lambert; 99: Collections; 101: SPL;
102: TR Mark Powell, M GSF, MR SPL; 103: Environmental
Images; 106: TR West Sussex Police, MR Peter Gould; 108:
TR Peter Gould, BR SPL; 109: SPL; 110: TR Andrew
Lambert, MR Andrew Lambert, BR Peter Gould; 111:
M Robert Harding, MR Roger Scruton; 112: four pictures
left to right Peter Gould, far right Andrew Lambert; 113:
TM Roger Scruton, TR Roger Scruton, MR SPL, BR SPL;
114: TR OSF, M ECON, BR Salt Union; 116: M Mary
Evans, TR Ace Photos, B Gerstenburg; 120: TR SPL, B Peter
Gould; 121: T Peter Gould, M Peter Gould; 122: T SPL,
B SPL; 124: TR Robert Harding, M Andrew Lambert,
MR Andrew Lambert, B Corbis; 126: TR Peter Gould,
B SPL; 128: TR AA & A, ML Anthony Blake, M Anthony
Blake, B Peter Gould; 129: SPL; 130: SPL; 131: Roger
Scruton; 132: M SPL; BL SPL; 136: M Robert Harding,
R OSF; 137: R Ann Fullick, M OSF; 139: TR SPL, ML Peter
Gould; 140: GSF; 141: SPL; 142: Peter Gould; 143: Ace
Photos; 144: TR Peter Gould, BR Mark Powell.

Picture research by Thelma Gilbert

The publishers have made every effort to trace the
copyright holders, but if they have inadvertently
overlooked any, they will be pleased to make the
necessary arrangements at the first opportunity.

AQA examination questions are reproduced by
permission of the Assessment and Qualifications Alliance.

Tel: 01865 888058   www.heinemann.co.uk

Introduction

Chemistry – the science which looks at matter and the way it behaves. The world of chemistry is intriguing and absorbing, and full of possibilities. In this book you will find out more about the behaviour of atoms and molecules, and how this behaviour affects and influences everything around us.

This book has been written to support you as you study the AQA Coordinated Science GCSE. As well as lots of facts and clear explanations with diagrams and photos to illustrate the science, there are some other features which will add interest and depth to your learning.

⊙ **Science people** introduces you to some of the scientists who have worked out the science we now take for granted.
⊙ **Ideas and evidence** looks at the way ideas about chemistry have developed and grown over the years.

At the end of each double page spread there are questions to help you check that you have understood the material you have just read, and at the end of each chapter there are GCSE style questions which will allow you to test your knowledge for the exams ahead.

Studying chemistry will give you an increased understanding of the world of materials – their properties, their uses and how new materials can be made. We hope this book will help you in your studies, and help you enjoy chemistry throughout your course.

Contents

Chapter 6: The periodic table

Chapter 7: Acids, bases and salts

Chapter 8: Reaction rates

Chapter 9: Energy and equilibria

Everywhere we look we are surrounded by materials of different types – wood, paper, plastics, metals, wool, skin, glass … the list seems almost endless. Look around the Earth on which we live, and the number and type of materials becomes mind-boggling.

Material make-up

All substances are made of **atoms**. As far as we know there are about 100 different types of atom which occur naturally in the universe, and all of the matter which exists is based on combinations of these different types of atom.

Some substances are made up of only one type of atom. These substances are known as **elements**. As there are only about 100 different types of atom, there are only about 100 different elements.

Elements show an enormous range in properties. For example metals like copper, silver, zinc and gold are shiny solids with properties which are easily recognised. Other elements, like oxygen, nitrogen and chlorine, are non-metals and gases.

↑ **Figure 1:** The range of materials on Earth is vast. Chemistry helps us to make sense of it all!

aluminium

bromine

← **Figure 2:** A substance which contains only one sort of atom is an element.

↓ **Figure 3:** Almost everything in this picture is a compound, made up of a combination of atoms from several different elements.

Compounds

The vast majority of substances around us and in the universe are not pure elements. Most substances are made up of combinations of different types of atoms and are known as **compounds**. These range from simple combinations of two different elements such as water (hydrogen and oxygen combined) through to huge compounds made up of many atoms such as plastics and the genetic material, DNA. The arrangement of nearly 100 elements in different combinations means that there is an almost infinite variety of materials.

The structure of atoms

All elements are made up of atoms. Because compounds are made up of elements, it follows that all compounds are made up of atoms too. In the middle of an atom is a small nucleus which contains two types of particles, called protons and neutrons. A third type of particle is found orbiting the nucleus – the electron. Every atom has the same number of electrons orbiting its nucleus as it has protons in its nucleus.

The mass of a proton and a neutron are the same. Another way of putting this is to say that the **relative mass** of a neutron compared to a proton is 1. Electrons are far, far smaller than protons and neutrons – their relative mass is negligible. Because of this, the mass of an atom is concentrated in its nucleus – the electrons in an atom just do not matter when it comes to thinking about its mass!

However, the electrons are important when it comes to thinking about charge. Protons have a positive charge while neutrons have no charge – they are neutral – so the nucleus itself has an overall positive charge. The electrons orbiting the nucleus are negatively charged. The size of the negative charge on an electron is exactly the same as the size of the positive charge on a proton. (In other words, the **relative charge** on a proton is +1, while the relative charge on an electron is −1.) Because any atom contains equal numbers of protons and electrons, the overall charge on any atom is exactly zero. For example, a carbon atom has six protons, so we know it also has six electrons. Similarly oxygen has eight protons and therefore eight electrons.

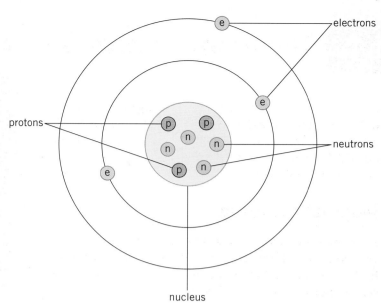

↑ **Figure 4:** Understanding the structure of an atom gives us vital clues to the way chemicals react together.

Type of sub-atomic particle	Relative mass	Relative charge
proton	1	+1
neutron	1	0
electron	negligible	−1

? Questions

1 What is an element?

2 **a** What is the difference between an element and a compound?

   b Why are there so many more compounds than there are elements?

3 **a** An atom has two protons and two neutrons in its nucleus. Draw a diagram of this atom to show protons, neutrons and electrons.

   b How do you know how many electrons to draw in orbit around this atom?

4 **a** Iron atoms have 26 protons. How many electrons would you expect?

   b Zinc atoms have 30 electrons moving around the nucleus. How many protons would you expect there to be in the nucleus?

   c A special type of atom known as carbon-14 has six protons and eight neutrons. How many electrons would you expect?

Key Ideas

⊙ All matter is made up of atoms.

⊙ Elements are substances made up of only one type of atom.

⊙ Atoms have a central nucleus which contains protons and neutrons.

⊙ Electrons move in orbits around the nucleus.

⊙ Protons have a relative mass of 1 and a positive charge.

⊙ Neutrons have a relative mass of 1 and are neutral.

⊙ Electrons have negligible mass and a negative charge.

Ideas about atoms

All substances are made up of atoms. We all accept this, yet no one has ever seen an atom in detail. Atoms are so small it would take billions of them to cover a single full stop! The closest we come to seeing atoms is when a scanning electron microscope is used to magnify metal structures many thousands of times.

How did our model of the atom evolve?

We take the existence of atoms for granted – yet for centuries no one believed in them. Around 2500 years ago a Greek philosopher called Leucippus and his pupil Demokritos put forward the idea that the universe is made up of tiny indivisible particles, which they called atoms. Unfortunately the great Greek philosopher Aristotle did not agree with them. As Aristotle's views were accepted throughout Europe for almost 2000 years the idea of atoms was shelved for centuries to come.

The problem with the idea of atoms is that there is no easily available evidence for their existence. In fact, common sense says that solids are solid and liquids are liquid, not lots of tiny particles which no one can see.

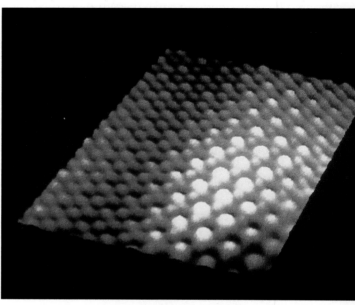

↑ **Figure 1:** Palladium atoms within the crystal lattice structure of the metal. These fuzzy blobs are the closest we have yet come to seeing individual atoms. This photograph was taken using a scanning electron microscope.

John Dalton's atomic theory

About 200 years ago an English scientist named John Dalton was working on the nature of gases and chemical compounds. As a result of observations he had made during his experiments he published a ground-breaking theory on the nature of matter. He suggested that:

- All matter is made up of indivisible particles called atoms.
- Atoms of the same element are similar in mass and shape but differ from the atoms of other elements.
- Atoms cannot be created or destroyed.
- Atoms join together to form compound atoms (what we now call molecules) in simple ratios.

Dalton's statements were backed up with much research. Even though not all of it was accurate – for example he thought that one hydrogen atom combined with one oxygen atom to form water – most of it reflected the same results as other scientists of the time were getting. Dalton's atomic theory explained much of what scientists were seeing, and so this time around the idea of atoms was accepted relatively quickly. Some scientists even made wooden models of atoms of different elements, to show their different relative sizes.

Not everyone was an immediate fan however – one critic wrote 'Atoms are round bits of wood invented by Mr Dalton'! But by 1850, the atomic theory of matter was almost universally accepted and virtually all opposition had disappeared. Dalton's atomic theory was the basis of much of the chemistry done in the rest of the 19th and early 20th century.

John Dalton was born in 1766 in the Lake District in England. His father was a weaver, and he taught John before sending him to a Quaker school in Eaglesfield, the town where they lived. John was incredibly bright, and was teaching other people by the time he was 12 years old! His interests were far ranging. He made many original observations on the weather – over 57 years he built up around 200 000 observations and measurements of the weather in the Manchester area! He was also the first person to identify and study colour blindness – his interest stemmed from the fact that he was colour blind himself. But Dalton is best remembered for his ideas in chemistry, particularly his atomic theory of matter which was published in 1808 in a book titled 'A New System of Chemical Philosophy'. Although his work was not perfectly accurate, it became the basis of the modern periodic table. Dalton also discovered a law governing the behaviour of a mixture of gases – he was indeed a worthy winner of the Gold Medal given by the Royal Society in 1882.

↑ **Figure 2:** John Dalton – the man who gave us atoms!

Ideas and Evidence

Developing the atomic model

Clear ideas of what an atom might actually be didn't start to emerge until around the beginning of the 20th century. In 1897 Joseph John Thompson showed that electrons were found in all matter. He also came up with a model for the atom, suggesting that the negative electrons were embedded in a sphere of positive charge like dried fruit in a 'plum pudding'. Then in 1911 Ernest Rutherford and his colleagues showed that the plum pudding model was wrong. Rutherford's model atom had a nucleus with electrons moving around it in orbits like the planets orbiting the sun.

In 1932 the British scientist James Chadwick carried out experiments which showed that neutrons, the final atomic particle to be discovered, actually existed. The changes that have been made to the model in the 70-odd years since are all relatively minor – our working model of the atom comes from almost a century ago.

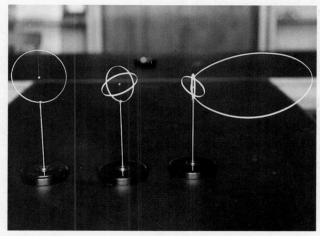

↑ **Figure 3:** Some early models of the nuclear atom.

Questions

1 Why was the idea of atoms rejected for over 200 years?

2 Why was Dalton's theory that matter is made up of atoms accepted relatively easily?

3 When people accepted Dalton's theory that all matter is made up of atoms they began to try and build up a model of what an atom looks like. Describe three different models of the atom which have been accepted at various times.

4 How have scientists built up a model of atoms without being able to see them?

H

5 Investigate the evidence built up by J J Thompson for his model of the atom and also the evidence on which Ernest Rutherford built up his model of atomic structure.

Key Ideas

⊙ John Dalton's atomic theory was accepted because it helped to explain what many other scientists were observing at the time.

Atomic number

The number of protons in the nucleus of an atom is known as its **atomic number** or **proton number**. As all the atoms of a particular element have the same number of protons they also have the same atomic number. So the atomic number of hydrogen is 1 and it has 1 proton in the nucleus, the atomic number of carbon is 6 and it has 6 protons in the nucleus, and the atomic number of sodium is 11 and it has 11 protons in the nucleus.

Each element has its own atomic number. If you are told that the atomic number of an element is 8, you can identify that element from tables of data or the periodic table – in this case it is oxygen.

Mass number

Almost all of the mass of an atom is found in the nucleus, because the mass of the electrons is so small it is negligible. The total number of protons and neutrons in an atom is known as the **mass number**.

When we want to show the atomic number and mass number of an atom it is done like this:

mass number   12

$$^{12}_{6}\text{C} \text{ (carbon)} \qquad ^{23}_{11}\text{Na} \text{ (sodium)}$$

atomic number   6   11

The number of neutrons present in the nucleus of an atom can be worked out by subtracting the atomic number from the mass number – the difference is the number of neutrons:

     mass number – atomic number = number of neutrons

For the two examples given, carbon has 6 protons and a mass number of 12, so the number of neutrons is 12 – 6 = 6. Sodium, on the other hand, has an atomic number of 11 but the mass number is 23; 23 – 11 = 12, so in this sodium atom there are 11 protons and 12 neutrons.

Isotopes

Atoms of the same element always have the same number of protons, but they do not always have the same number of neutrons. Atoms of the same element with different numbers of neutrons are known as **isotopes**. For example, carbon has two common isotopes, $^{12}_{6}\text{C}$ (carbon-12) and $^{14}_{6}\text{C}$ (carbon-14). The carbon-12 isotope has 6 protons and 6 neutrons in the nucleus, whilst the carbon-14 isotope has 6 protons and 8 neutrons.

Sometimes the extra neutrons in its nucleus make the isotope unstable, so that it is radioactive. However not all isotopes are radioactive – they are simply atoms of the same substance with a different mass. Although different isotopes of the same element may have different *physical* properties (they have a different mass and they may be radioactive), they always have the same *chemical* properties. For example, hydrogen has three isotopes: hydrogen, deuterium and tritium. They have different masses and tritium is radioactive but they can all react with oxygen to make water.

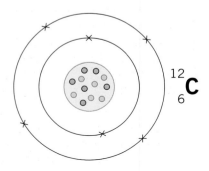

| proton | Number of protons gives atomic number. |
| neutron | Number of protons plus number of neutrons gives mass number. |

↑ **Figure 1:** The atomic number and the mass number of an element are useful tools to the chemist in many ways.

$^{1}_{1}\text{H}$ hydrogen

$^{2}_{1}\text{H}$ deuterium

$^{3}_{1}\text{H}$ tritium

↑ **Figure 2:** The isotopes of hydrogen – similar chemical properties, different physical properties.

Isotopes in science and medicine

Radioactive isotopes can be used to find out about the chemistry of living things because they can be traced with special detectors. For example, tritium enabled scientists to work out what happens as plants make food by photosynthesis. The scientists replaced ordinary hydrogen with tritium in some water molecules. These molecules were then taken up by the plants. The tritium could be traced to show how the water was broken down in photosynthesis.

In hospitals radioactive isotopes are often used to see what is happening inside a patient's body without having to cut it open. For example, the thyroid gland is the only part of the body which takes up iodine. So if you inject a patient with radioactive iodine it can be traced to help you see how the thyroid is working.

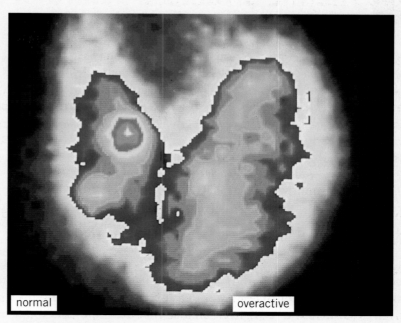

normal   overactive

↑ **Figure 3:** The difference between normal thyroid tissue and thyroid tissue which is overactive can be seen clearly using special isotopes of iodine.

1 What is the difference between the atomic (or proton) number and the mass number?

2 Write each of the elements below in the following way:

   mass number   12
   symbol for element, eg   **C**
   atomic number   6

   a helium, mass number 4, atomic number 2

   b calcium, mass number 40, atomic number 20

   c oxygen, mass number 16, atomic number 8.

3 For each of the following elements give the mass number and state how many protons and neutrons would be found in the nucleus. Show your working.

   a $^9_4$Be

   b $^{24}_{12}$Mg

   c $^{80}_{35}$Br

   d $^{19}_9$F

   e $^{197}_{79}$Au

4 **a** What is an isotope?

   b How may the physical properties of isotopes of the same element vary?

5 How are radioactive isotopes used in research and medicine?

⊙ The number of protons in the nucleus is known as the atomic number or proton number.

⊙ The number of protons and neutrons is known as the mass number.

⊙ Atoms of the same element always have the same number of protons and electrons.

⊙ Two atoms of the same element with different numbers of neutrons are known as isotopes.

⊙ The isotopes of an element may have different physical properties but they will always have the same chemical properties.

Once the nuclear model for the atom was accepted, the next puzzle for scientists to solve was the behaviour of the electrons outside the nucleus. It seemed that it was the arrangement of the electrons which affected how different atoms reacted – but a model which explained all the observed properties of the different elements was not easy to find.

Energy levels

The model of the atom which scientists now use has electrons arranged around the nucleus in **shells**, rather like the layers of an onion. Each shell is at a different **energy level**, the lowest energy level being the one which is nearest to the nucleus.

With their negative charge, electrons are attracted to the positively charged nucleus. To move an electron from a shell close to the nucleus to one further away therefore requires energy, to overcome this attractive force. This means that electrons in shells further away from the nucleus have more energy than electrons in shells closer to the nucleus. To remind us about the importance of energy levels in atoms, from now on we shall always use the term *energy level* when we talk about the arrangement of electrons in atoms.

← **Figure 1:** No one has actually seen electrons in their different energy levels around the nucleus of an atom, but with the aid of computers people have come up with some fairly spectacular models!

We could not possibly represent atoms as they are shown in Figure 1 every time we need to show the structure of an atom, so for simplicity they are usually drawn as in Figure 2.

An energy level can only hold a certain number of electrons. The first, and lowest energy level holds two electrons. The second and third levels are each filled by eight electrons. Once there are eight electrons in the third energy level, the fourth begins to fill up, and so on. Atoms where the outer energy level is full are very stable and unreactive. They are called the **noble gases** – helium, neon and argon are examples.

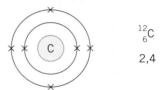

$^{12}_{6}C$

2,4

↑ **Figure 2:** A simple way of representing the electrons in an atom and the energy levels where they are found. This is sometimes called the *electronic configuration* of the atom. A carbon atom is shown here.

The most common way of showing the arrangement of electrons in an atom is to draw diagrams like those in Figure 2 and to write down the numbers of electrons in each energy level. The atomic number of an element tells us how many electrons there are in the atoms. For example, for the carbon atom in Figure 2 the atomic number is 6, giving us six electrons. We write its electronic structure as 2,4. So an atom with the atomic number 12 has an electronic structure 2,8,2, with two electrons in the inner energy level, then eight in the next energy level and two in the outer, highest energy level. The simplest way to understand these arrangements is to look at lots of examples of them.

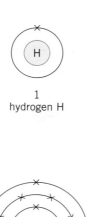

1
hydrogen H

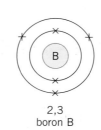

2,3
boron B

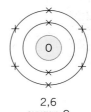

2,6
oxygen O

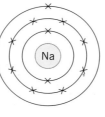

2,8,1
sodium Na

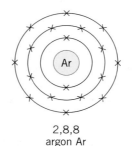

2,8,8
argon Ar

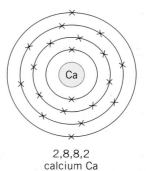

2,8,8,2
calcium Ca

↑ **Figure 3:** Once we know the pattern we can draw the energy levels of the electrons in any atom we choose.

? **Questions**

1 Why do the electrons in the shell closest to the nucleus have least energy?

2 Which group of elements have full outer energy shells?

3 Identify each of the elements shown below and give the atomic number and the electronic structure numerically.

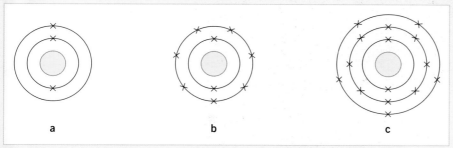

      a   b   c

4 a Draw diagrams to show the energy shells and give the numerical electronic structure for the following elements.

   i helium (atomic number 2)

   ii nitrogen (atomic number 7)

  iii neon (atomic number 10)

  iv sulphur (atomic number 16)

   v potassium (atomic number 19)

  vi chlorine (atomic number 17)

 vii aluminium (atomic number 13)

viii beryllium (atomic number 4)

  ix magnesium (atomic number 12)

 b What is special about the arrangement of helium, neon and argon?

O—m **Key Ideas**

⊙ Electrons are arranged around the nucleus in shells.

⊙ Each shell is at a different energy level.

⊙ The lowest energy level is closest to the nucleus; the highest energy level is furthest away from the nucleus.

⊙ Different energy levels can hold different numbers of electrons.

All matter is made up of atoms, but even the same types of matter can sometimes look very different because they can exist in more than one state – as a solid, a liquid or a gas. Understanding these different states is an important part of chemistry.

Changing state

In Figure 1 the solid water in the icicle is forming drips of liquid water as it melts in the warmth of the sun – it is changing state. Changes of state involve energy changes.

The particles in all substances are vibrating (moving), even if the movement is very slight, unless they are at absolute zero (−273 °C), when all movement stops. If energy is put into a solid, for example by heating, its particles will vibrate more violently. If enough energy is supplied the particles may move further away from each other and become freer to move around. At this point the material changes state from a solid to a liquid – it melts. The temperature at which any solid substance melts is known as its **melting point**.

On the other hand, if energy is lost from a liquid then the particles slow down and move closer together again. The attractive forces which hold particles together in a solid then form again, and the liquid becomes solid – this takes place at the **freezing point** of the liquid.

If a liquid is heated the particles within it will move around faster and faster. Eventually some of the particles will have enough energy to overcome the attractive forces between them and the rest of the particles. They will escape from the liquid and become a gas. This is known as **evaporation**. As the temperature gets higher, more particles have enough energy to escape so evaporation gets faster and faster until big bubbles of gas form in the liquid and it begins to boil. The temperature at which this happens is known as the **boiling point**.

In the reverse situation, if a gas loses energy to the surroundings then the particles may move much more slowly and become closely packed again, forming a liquid – this is **condensation**.

↑ **Figure 1:** Solid water (ice), with liquid water, surrounded by air containing gaseous water – the three states of matter.

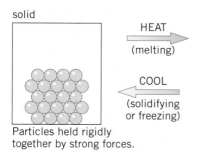

solid

HEAT
(melting)

COOL
(solidifying or freezing)

Particles held rigidly together by strong forces.

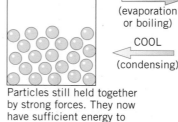

liquid

HEAT
(evaporation or boiling)

COOL
(condensing)

Particles still held together by strong forces. They now have sufficient energy to move about, but cannot escape from one another.

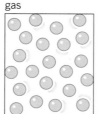

gas

Particles now have enough energy to move apart, overcoming attractive forces holding them together. The particles move freely throughout the container.

← **Figure 2:** Changing state involves changing amounts of energy and differences in the movements of the particles making up matter.

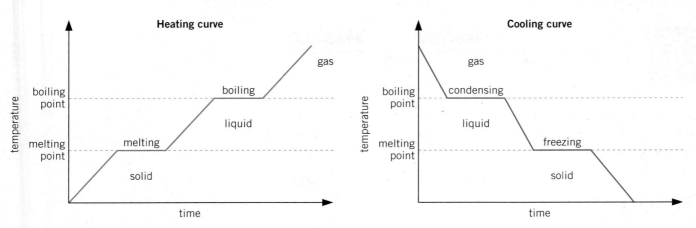

↑ **Figure 3:** As substances change state the heat energy is used to break the forces of attraction between particles instead of raising the temperature, so when things melt, boil, condense or freeze the temperature stays the same.

1 The table shows melting and boiling points for some elements.

Element	Melting point (°C)	Boiling point (°C)
carbon	3652	4827
oxygen	−218	−183
sodium	98	883
mercury	−39	357
aluminium	660	2467

a What state will the following elements be in at a temperature of 95 °C?

   i mercury   ii oxygen   iii aluminium   iv sodium

b What state will the following elements be in at 500 °C?

   i carbon   ii mercury   iii sodium   iv aluminium

2 Some elements melt at much higher temperatures than others – for example copper melts at 1084 °C whilst iron melts at 1535 °C. Other elements are gases all the time at normal room temperature. What does this tell you about the strength of the forces between the particles in different elements? Explain your answer.

3 The data in the table were collected when a colourless liquid was being heated.

a Make a graph of the data.

b Explain what is happening:

   i when the temperature of the graph is increasing

   ii when the temperature of the graph becomes constant.

c Suggest what the colourless liquid might be and explain your answer.

Time (min)	Temperature (°C)
1	20
2	35
3	50
4	65
5	80
6	95
7	100
8	100
9	100

Key Ideas

⊙ In a solid, the particles are held tightly together so they may vibrate but they cannot change position – solids have a definite shape.

⊙ In a liquid the particles are held less tightly together, although they are about the same distance apart as in a solid – liquids have no fixed shape.

⊙ The particles in a gas are widely separated compared to the particles in a liquid – unlike liquids and solids, gases can be compressed, and they expand to fill the container in which they are placed.

⊙ Changing state involves energy being supplied to or removed from a substance.

The atoms of the chemical elements are the basis of all the chemistry in the world around us. These elements, and the symbols we use to represent them, are like the alphabet of a very specialised language. But like any other language, the alphabet alone is of little use. What really matters is the way the different letters are used together to produce words. In the same way in chemistry, what matters is the way the different elements are combined together to make new chemical compounds.

Mixing or making

Everyone knows that two substances can be mixed together without either of them changing. Sand and salt can be mixed and then separated again, and no change will have taken place. Sugar can be dissolved in tea and separated out again. But in *chemical reactions* the situation is very different. When the atoms of two (or more) elements react, they make a chemical which is different to both of them and you cannot get either of them back.

Compounds can also react together to form other compounds, but the reaction of elements is easier to understand as a starting point.

↑ Figure 1: Chemical reactions may be awe-inspiringly spectacular or relatively mundane. Whatever they are like, they involve the joining of the atoms of different elements to make another chemical.

mixing

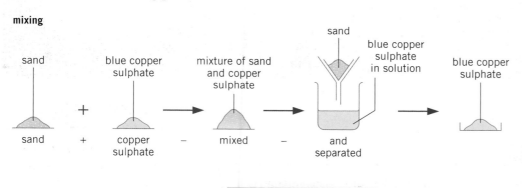

sand + copper sulphate − mixed − and separated

reacting

2Na + Cl$_2$ ⟶ reaction ⟶ 2NaCl

↖ Figure 2: The difference between mixing and reacting can be dramatic!

Explaining covalent properties

Covalent bonds are very strong – the atoms within the covalent molecules are held very tightly together. However, each molecule tends to be quite separate, and the attraction between the individual molecules in a covalent compound tends to be small. The small attractive forces between the molecules (weak intermolecular forces) and the fact that covalent molecules do not carry an overall electric charge means that it takes relatively little energy to separate them, and this results in the low melting points and boiling points of covalent compounds.

As a result, covalent compounds which consist of individual molecules are gases at room temperature and pressure – carbon dioxide and sulphur dioxide are examples – or liquids with relatively low boiling points, such as water.

Many other covalent compounds are solids with low melting points, but a small number have a very different structure. They form giant structures where huge numbers of atoms are held together because they are sharing electrons. These giant molecular structures are lattices made up of molecules, and covalent bonds hold the structure together. Because covalent bonds are very strong, these covalent compounds tend to be very hard with very high melting points – very different from the majority of covalent compounds. Good examples of these structures are carbon in the form of diamond and graphite, and silicon dioxide (silica).

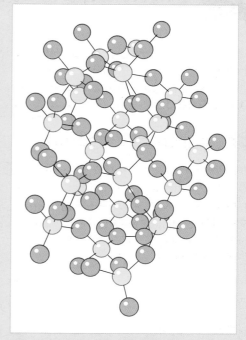

↑ **Figure 6:** A giant covalent lattice of silicon and oxygen atoms (silica).

? Questions

1 With the help of the data at the back of the book, work out the electronic structure of the following non-metals. For each one, state how many electrons it would need to share in a covalent bond.

 a nitrogen (N)

 b sulphur (S)

 c fluorine (F)

 d phosphorus (P)

2 Draw dot and cross diagrams to show the following reactions.

 a carbon + oxygen ⟶ carbon dioxide

 b sulphur + chlorine ⟶ sulphur chloride

 c hydrogen + fluorine ⟶ hydrogen fluoride

3 Represent the covalent bonds in each of the following molecules in three different ways.

 a hydrogen chloride (HCl)

 b oxygen (O_2)

 c hydrogen (H_2)

 d methane (CH_4)

H 4 The melting point of sand (silicon dioxide) is more than 1600 °C, while the melting point of ice is 0 °C. Both of these are covalent compounds. Explain the difference in their melting points.

🔑 Key Ideas

- ⊙ Atoms in molecules are held together by covalent bonds.

- ⊙ A covalent bond is formed when two atoms share electrons between them to gain the electronic structure of a noble gas.

- ⊙ Substances made up of molecules containing covalent bonds have low melting and boiling points.

- ⊙ Giant covalent structures are held together by covalent bonds.

H ⊙ The properties of giant covalent structures differ from those of molecular covalent structures.

Ionic compounds can also form **giant structures** – arrangements of atoms or ions that extend over large distances.

Ionic solids

The ions within an ionic compound are held together by forces of mutual attraction in a seemingly endless array known as a giant ionic lattice. The arrangement of ions within these lattices always forms a regular pattern.

The strong forces between the oppositely charged ions in giant ionic lattices result in high melting and boiling points for the compounds.

Another property of ionic compounds is that once they are dissolved in water or melted, they conduct electricity. The charged ions become free to move and so can carry charge through the liquid. In the solid state ionic substances do not conduct electricity because the ions are held in the rigid giant lattice structure.

More about covalent structures

As we saw in Section 1.8 a small number of covalent compounds also have giant structures. Covalent giant structures are held together by covalent bonds which give them unusually high melting points and hardness for covalent structures. Diamonds are well known for their hardness and their stability – they react with very little. These characteristics are the result of the chemical bonding within the giant molecular structure which makes up a diamond. Each carbon atom forms four covalent bonds with its neighbours in a rigid giant covalent lattice (Figure 2).

Carbon doesn't always turn up as diamonds – another form is graphite (well known as the lead in your pencils!). In graphite each carbon atom forms three covalent bonds so the carbon atoms form layers or sheets which can slide freely over each other. This is another type of giant covalent lattice.

Another important characteristic of graphite comes from the fact that there are free electrons within the structure. These free electrons, which are not directly involved in covalent bonds, allow graphite to conduct electricity, which diamond – and most other covalent compounds – cannot do.

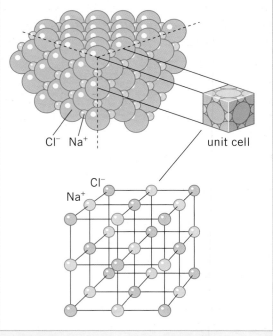

↑ Figure 1: The regular patterns of giant ionic lattices affect their physical properties – this is sodium chloride again.

↓ Figure 2: Diamonds owe their hardness and long-lasting nature to the way the carbon molecules are arranged.

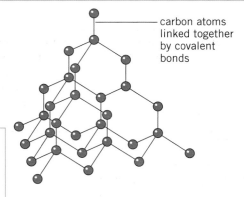

carbon atoms linked together by covalent bonds

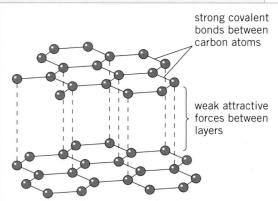

strong covalent bonds between carbon atoms

weak attractive forces between layers

↑ Figure 3: The giant structure of graphite. When you write with a pencil, some layers of carbon atoms slide off the 'lead' and are left on the paper.

Metals

Metals are yet other examples of giant structures. You can think of metal as a lattice of metal atoms which have each given up one or more of their outer electrons. This means that they become positively charged (remember that a charged atom is called an ion). The electrons they give up form a 'sea' of free electrons surrounding the positive metal ions. The negatively charged electrons attract the positively charged metal ions and hold them together just like glue.

However, unlike glue the electrons are able to move throughout the whole lattice. Because they can move and hold the metal ions together at the same time, the free electrons enable the lattice to distort so that the metal ions can move past one another. This means that it is possible to hammer metals into shape and to draw them out into wires.

Metal cooking utensils are used the world over, because metals are good conductors of heat. Wherever electricity is generated, metal wires carry the electricity to where it is needed, because metals are also good conductors of electricity. Both of these properties are a direct result of the ability of electrons to flow through the sea of free electrons surrounding the metal atoms in the giant metal lattice.

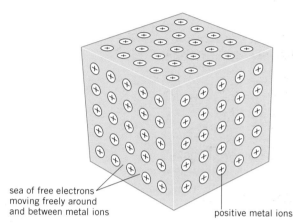

sea of free electrons moving freely around and between metal ions

positive metal ions

↖ **Figure 4:** People have shaped and used metals for thousands of years – making horseshoes is a skill that is centuries old. The ability of metals to be shaped in this way is dependent on a giant lattice structure of positive metal ions surrounded by free electrons.

? Questions

1 Explain why substances consisting of giant structures usually have high melting and boiling points.

2 Copy and complete the table.

Substance	Melting point (°C)	Boiling point (°C)	Conducts electricity at room temperature?	Conducts electricity when liquid?	Structure (giant ionic / giant covalent / giant metal / covalent molecular)
quartz (silicon dioxide)	1610	2230			
rubidium fluoride	795	1410			
manganese	1244	1962			
sulphur dioxide	−73	−10			

3 Why can ionic compounds conduct electricity when they melt or are in solution?

4 Why can graphite and metals conduct electricity?

5 Why can you write with graphite?

⊙⊓ Key Ideas

- ⊙ Giant structures consist of large numbers of atoms or ions arranged in a regular array.
- ⊙ Ionic compounds have giant ionic lattices in which the strong forces between oppositely charged ions hold the ions tightly together.
- ⊙ Giant covalent structures are held together by covalent bonds.
- ⊙ Giant metal structures are held together by free electrons which hold the lattice of metal atoms together.

1 a Methane and propane are two fuels. The diagrams represent a molecule of each.

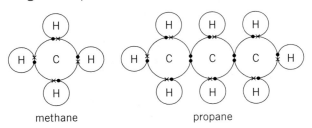

methane   propane

   i Which is the correct formula for methane?

     CH   CH$_2$ CH$_3$ CH$_4$ (1 mark)

   ii Which is the correct formula for propane?

     CH$_8$ C$_2$H$_8$ C$_3$H$_8$ C$_8$H$_8$ (1 mark)

   iii Both methane and propane have covalent bonds. Copy the sentence below, choosing the correct word from the list to complete it.

     exchanged   gained   lost   shared

     In covalent bonds, the electrons from each atom are ....   (1 mark)

b **i** When coal is burnt the sulphur it contains is changed into sulphur dioxide (SO$_2$). The reaction is shown in the equation

     S(s) + O$_2$(g) $\longrightarrow$ SO$_2$(g)

     Which word describes the state of the sulphur dioxide?

     aqueous   gas   liquid   solid   (1 mark)

   ii What does the formula SO$_2$ tell you about a molecule of sulphur dioxide?   (2 marks)

                      (Total 6 marks)

             AQA specimen question

2 a The diagram shows the atomic structure of an atom of lithium.

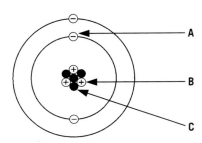

   i The atom contains electrons, neutrons and protons. Which type of particle is labelled **A**, **B** and **C**?   (2 marks)

   ii What is the atomic number of lithium?

                               (1 mark)

b The diagrams show the electron arrangement of the atoms of two elements.

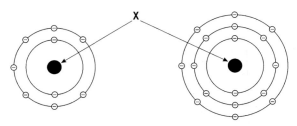

   i Name the part of the atoms labelled **X**.   (1 mark)

   ii What is the significance of the rings around part **X**?   (2 marks)

                      (Total 6 marks)

             AQA specimen question

(H) 3 a The structural formula of a hydrazine molecule is shown below.

Copy and complete the diagram to show how the outer energy level (shell) electrons are arranged in a hydrazine molecule. Show the electrons as dots and crosses.   (2 marks)

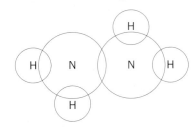

b Explain why hydrazine has a low boiling point.   (2 marks)

                      (Total 4 marks)

             AQA specimen question

H **4** Silicon has a structure similar to diamond.

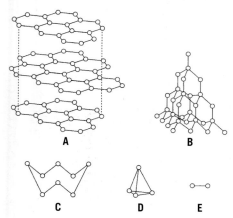

a Which of the diagrams, **A** to **E**, represents the structure of silicon? (1 mark)

b Explain why silicon has a very high melting point. (2 marks)
(Total 3 marks)
AQA specimen question

5 The diagrams labelled **A** to **D** are atoms of four different elements. The elements are oxygen ($^{16}_{8}O$), carbon ($^{12}_{6}C$), sodium ($^{23}_{11}Na$) and neon ($^{20}_{10}Ne$).

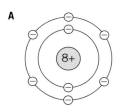
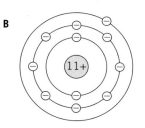
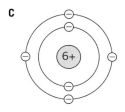
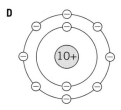

a Identify each atom, **A** to **D**, and for each one give its electronic structure. (4 marks)

b i What type of bonding would you expect in a reaction between elements **A** and **C**? (1 mark)

ii Draw a dot and cross diagram to show the reaction between these two elements. (2 marks)

c What type of bonding would you expect in a reaction between elements **A** and **B**? (1 mark)

ii Draw a dot and cross diagram to show the reaction between these two elements. (2 marks)

d Would you expect element **D** to react with element **A**? Explain your answer. (2 marks)
(Total 12 marks)

6 Explain in your own words, using good English, the difference between the following:

a elements and compounds (2 marks)

b mixtures and compounds (2 marks)

c atomic number and atomic mass. (2 marks)
(Total 6 marks)

7 The diagram represents the structure of a metal.

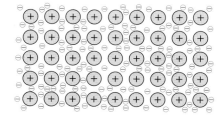

a Copy the sentence below, choosing the correct word from the list to complete it.

molecular   ionic   giant   strong

The arrangement of positive ions and a sea of electrons in a metal is an example of a .... structure. (1 mark)

b How does this structure explain:

i the high melting point of most metals (1 mark)

ii the fact that solid metals conduct electricity? (1 mark)

c How does the structure of an ionic substance like sodium chloride differ from the metallic structure shown here? (2 marks)

d How does the structure of a covalent substance like graphite differ from the metallic structure shown here? (2 marks)
(Total 7 marks)

2.1 Representing chemicals

When a chemical reaction takes place we can observe what happens and describe it, but to enable someone else to carry out the same reaction, that is simply not enough. 'Add 3 g of a white powder to $10\,cm^3$ of a colourless liquid' could have any number of outcomes, from nothing happening at all to a violent explosion.

Whether a chemical reaction takes place in a laboratory or a chemical factory, chemists need to be able to represent what happens on paper. What is more, they need to do this in a way which gives as much information as possible about what is going on.

↑ **Figure 1:** It is very important that once a chemical experiment has been carried out, other chemists can understand what has been done and try it for themselves.

Representing elements

The simplest way to describe chemical elements and compounds is to use their full names – water, copper sulphate, hydrochloric acid. But the names are different in different languages. Much scientific work is international so we use symbols for the elements which are understood and used across the whole world.

11 **B** boron 5	12 **C** carbon 6	14 **N** nitrogen 7	16 **O** oxygen 8	19 **F** fluorine 9	20 **Ne** neon 10
27 **Al** aluminium 13	28 **Si** silicon 14	31 **P** phosphorus 15	32 **S** sulphur 16	35 **Cl** chlorine 17	40 **Ar** argon 18
70 **Ga** gallium 31	73 **Ge** germanium 32	75 **As** arsenic 33	79 **Se** selenium 34	80 **Br** bromine 35	84 **Kr** krypton 36

← **Figure 2:** The periodic table gives you the international symbols for all of the commonly known elements and many others besides! (Only a part of it is shown here – the full version is given on page 88 and at the back of the book.)

Representing compounds

It is not only important for a chemist to know what elements make up a compound. A chemist also wants to know how many atoms of the different elements have combined together to form the compound. This is where chemical formulae are vital.

Appearance of compound	Name of compound	Chemical formula	What the formula means
	water	H_2O	2 atoms of hydrogen are combined with 1 atom of oxygen
	copper sulphate	$CuSO_4$	1 atom of copper, 1 atom of sulphur and 4 oxygen atoms are combined
	sodium chloride	NaCl	1 atom of sodium is combined with 1 atom of chlorine
	nitric acid	HNO_3	1 atom of hydrogen, 1 atom of nitrogen and 3 atoms of oxygen are combined

OXIDISING

These substances provide oxygen which allows other materials to burn more fiercely. *Examples*: potassium manganate(VII) ($KMnO_4$), hydrogen peroxide (H_2O_2).

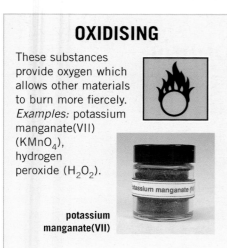

potassium manganate(VII)

TOXIC

These substances can cause death. They may have their effects when swallowed or breathed in or absorbed through the skin. *Examples*: mercury (Hg) and many of its compounds, lead (Pb) and many of its compounds.

mercury

HARMFUL

These substances are similar to toxic substances – they are poisonous – but they are less dangerous. *Examples*: lead(II) nitrate ($PbNO_3$), copper(II) chloride ($CuCl_2$).

copper(II) chloride

HIGHLY FLAMMABLE

These substances catch fire easily. *Examples*: methanol (CH_3OH), ethanol (C_2H_5OH), petrol.

ethanol

CORROSIVE

These substances attack and destroy living tissues, including eyes and skin. *Examples*: hydrochloric acid (HCl), sodium hydroxide (NaOH).

concentrated hydrochloric acid

IRRITANT

These substances are not corrosive but can cause reddening or blistering of the skin. *Example*: copper(II) oxide (CuO).

copper(II) oxide

↑ **Figure 3:** The six hazard symbols are recognised throughout the world.

Hazards in the home

The lab and industrial sites and vehicles are not the only places where chemical hazard symbols are used. In our homes we use a wide variety of chemicals which may be irritants, toxic, oxidising agents or have other potential risks. Hazardous substances are labelled with hazard symbols to warn us of the dangers. For example, household bleach carries the irritant symbol and methylated spirits are shown as highly flammable, while poisons designed to kill rats and mice have the toxic symbol on their packets. So for work in the lab and life outside the school or college gates, these symbols are worth remembering!

↑ **Figure 4:** Weedkillers containing chemicals like sodium chlorate are shown as harmful and oxidising agents.

? Questions

1 Either design a poster for the laboratory walls, showing the hazard symbols and explaining what they mean and why they are important,

or design a leaflet which could be given to each individual child when they start science lessons in year 7. Make sure that the leaflet is informative in a way they will understand but not so frightening that they refuse to enter the science labs.

Key Ideas

⊙ Some chemicals are particularly dangerous. They are labelled with special hazard symbols which are recognised internationally.

⊙ The six types of hazardous chemicals are oxidising, toxic, harmful, highly flammable, corrosive and irritant.

Chemical equations show you how many atoms you need of the reactants to make the products of a reaction. But when you are actually carrying out a chemical reaction you need to know what amounts to use in grams or cm^3. You might think that a chemical equation would also tell you this. For example, does the equation

$$Mg + 2HCl \longrightarrow MgCl_2 + H_2$$

mean that you need twice as much hydrochloric acid as magnesium to make magnesium chloride?

Unfortunately it isn't that simple, because the atoms of different elements have different masses. So, you need twice as many hydrogen and chlorine atoms as magnesium atoms, but this doesn't mean that the mass of hydrochloric acid will be twice the mass of magnesium. Atoms of different elements have different masses because each element contains a different number of protons and neutrons in the nucleus of its atoms.

To translate equations into something we can actually do in the lab or factory we have to know a bit more about the mass of atoms.

Relative atomic masses

The mass of a single atom is so tiny (a single hydrogen atom has a mass of less than $0.000\,000\,000\,000\,000\,000\,000\,002$ grams) that it would be incredibly awkward to use in calculations. To make the whole thing manageable scientists use a much simpler way of looking at the masses of atoms. Instead of working with the real masses of atoms, we focus on how the masses of atoms of different elements compare with each other.

How did this method come about? The first step was to choose a **standard atom**. The original choice was hydrogen, but it was finally decided that an atom of carbon ($^{12}_{6}C$) would be used as the standard. It was given a 'mass' of 12 units, because it has six protons and six neutrons. The masses of the atoms of all the other elements were then compared to the standard carbon atom, using a mass spectrometer. The mass of an atom found by comparing it to the $^{12}_{6}C$ atom is known as its **relative atomic mass (A_r)**.

The relative atomic mass of an element is usually the same as, or very similar to, the mass number of that element. The A_r takes into account any isotopes of the element – it is the average mass of the isotopes of the element in the proportions they are usually found, compared to the standard carbon atom.

When atoms change into ions they either lose or gain electrons. However, for all practical purposes the mass of electrons isn't worth bothering about, so the **relative ionic mass** of an ion is exactly the same as the relative atomic mass of that element.

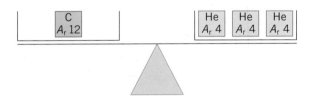

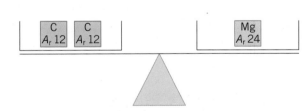

↑ **Figure 1:** The A_r for carbon is 12. Compared to this, the A_r for helium is 4, and for magnesium, 24.

Relative atomic mass		Relative ionic mass	
Na	23	Na$^+$	23
O	16	O^{2-}	16
Mg	24	Mg^{2+}	24

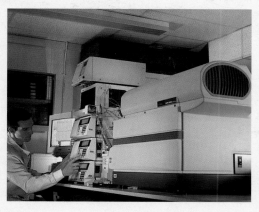
Relative formula masses

We can use the A_r of the various elements to work out the **relative formula mass** (M_r) of chemical compounds, whether they are made up of molecules or collections of ions.

A simple example is a substance like sodium chloride. We know that the A_r of sodium is 23 and of chlorine is 35.5. The formula mass of sodium chloride (NaCl) is:

$$23 + 35.5 = 58.5$$

A_r Na A_r Cl M_r NaCl

Another example is water. Water is made up of hydrogen and oxygen. The A_r of hydrogen is 1, and of oxygen is 16. Water has the formula H_2O, containing two hydrogen atoms for every one oxygen, so the M_r is:

$$(1 \times 2) + 16 = 18$$

A_r H $\times$ 2 A_r O M_r H_2O

The same approach works even with relatively complicated molecules like sulphuric acid, H_2SO_4. Hydrogen has an A_r of 1, sulphur of 32 and oxygen 16. This means that the M_r of sulphuric acid is:

$$(1 \times 2) + 32 + (16 \times 4) = 2 + 32 + 64 = 98$$

? Questions

1 Using the data at the back of the book, find the relative atomic masses of the following elements and ions.

  a Li   **b** S   **c** Ca^{2+} **d** Al   **e** F^- **f** N

2 There are two isotopes of chlorine. Three out of every four chlorine atoms have a mass of 35. One out of every four has a mass of 37. Use this information to work out the relative atomic mass of chlorine (the average mass of all the isotopes). Use the data at the back of the book to check your answer.

3 Use the data at the back of the book to help you work out the relative formula mass of the following compounds.

  a MgO   **b** NH_3 **c** $ZnSO_4$ **d** Cl_2 **e** CH_4 **f** $Mg(NO_3)_2$

🔑 Key Ideas

⊙ The relative atomic mass A_r of an element is the average mass of its isotopes compared with an atom of $^{12}_{6}C$.

⊙ The relative formula mass M_r of a compound is the sum of the relative atomic masses of all the atoms or ions which make up the chemical compound.

← **Figure 1:** Spectacular patterns in the Earth's surface – but how can we find out if these rocks contain minerals that can be extracted and used?

We can use the formula mass of a compound to calculate the percentage mass of each element in it. Calculations like this are not just done in GCSE chemistry exams! In life outside the school laboratory, geologists and mining companies base their decisions about whether to exploit mineral finds on calculations like those shown here.

Working out the amount of an element in a compound

We can use the relative atomic mass (A_r) of elements and the relative formula mass (M_r) of compounds to help us work out the percentage of an element in a compound. For example, what percentage by mass of white magnesium oxide is actually magnesium, and how much is oxygen?

The first thing we need is the formula of magnesium oxide, MgO. The A_r of magnesium is 24 g, whilst the A_r of oxygen is 16 g. Adding these together gives us an M_r of 40 g. We know that 24 g out of that 40 g is actually magnesium:

$$\frac{\text{mass of magnesium}}{\text{total mass of compound}} = \frac{24}{40}$$

So the percentage of magnesium in the compound is:

$$\frac{24}{40} \times 100 = 60\%$$

To calculate the percentage of an element in a compound

⊙ Write down the formula of the compound.

⊙ Using the relative atomic masses from the data at the back of the book, work out the relative formula mass M_r of the compound. Write down the mass of each element making up the compound as you work it out.

⊙ Write the mass of the element you are investigating as a fraction of the total M_r.

⊙ Find the percentage by multiplying your fraction by 100.

Getting rid of plastics

Plastics are light, cheap and often longer lasting than natural materials. This is why these artificial polymers produced from oil are so popular. However, there are some problems arising from the same properties which make plastics so useful.

Most plastics are incredibly long-lasting. They do not disintegrate naturally and they are not broken down by the microorganisms which cause all living material to decay. In other words they are not **biodegradable**. When we get rid of plastic rubbish it goes to the rubbish tips with all the rest of our household waste, but unlike everything else the plastic will still be there 10, 50 and even 100 years from now. The build-up of waste plastic will have serious consequences for the environment.

Almost all plastics will burn, so we could get rid of them by incineration. Unfortunately most plastics also produce toxic gases when they burn, which pollute the atmosphere and are a serious risk both to human health and to other living things.

At the moment there seem to be two approaches which may solve the problem of plastic disposal in the future.

⊙ **Recycling:** Some plastics can be melted down and reused. More and more people save the plastic bottles used for fizzy drinks, ketchup etc and take them to collection points for recycling. It only works for some types of plastic, but even plastic bits of cars are now recycled. As more and more plastic is collected and recycled, less and less oil has to be used to make new polymers and less plastic builds up in the environment.

⊙ **Biodegradable plastics:** More and more new polymers are being developed which can be broken down by bacteria – they are biodegradable. This means that when they are dumped they will eventually be broken down naturally. Even if they take a long time to break down, at least it holds out the hope that our grandchildren will not be living in the middle of the plastic waste we produce today.

↑ **Figure 3:** Plastic rubbish can be now found all over the world, carried by wind and water even to places where no people live – and the problem is simply not going to disappear.

3.5 Hydrocarbon chemistry

The compounds making up crude oil are called hydrocarbons. As the name suggests, hydrocarbons are made up of the elements hydrogen and carbon. They all have a spine of carbon atoms, with the hydrogen atoms attached around the spine. Although they all contain the same basic elements, hydrocarbons vary enormously in their properties and reactions. They form families of compounds, and each family has similar bonds in the carbon spine. The study of these families of hydrocarbons makes up part of the study of **organic chemistry**.

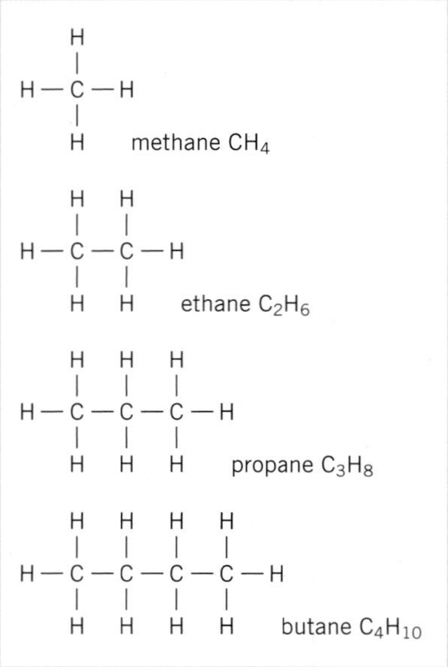

The alkanes

The simplest family of hydrocarbons is the **alkanes**. In this family the carbon atoms are joined by single covalent carbon–carbon bonds. All of the remaining bonds are carbon–hydrogen bonds. The alkanes are found in the lightest, gaseous fraction of crude oil.

When hydrocarbons are named, the final part of the name indicates which family of compounds the compound belongs to. In this case the ending **–ane** indicates an alkane. The prefix tells us how many carbon atoms there are in the molecule:

Prefix	Number of carbon atoms
Meth-	1
Eth-	2
Prop-	3
But-	4
Pent-	5

One important reaction of the alkanes is that they burn in air to give a considerable amount of heat. For this reason they are important as fuels.

$$\text{methane} + \text{oxygen} \longrightarrow \text{carbon dioxide} + \text{water}$$
$$CH_4 + 2O_2 \longrightarrow CO_2 + 2H_2O$$

$$\text{propane} + \text{oxygen} \longrightarrow \text{carbon dioxide} + \text{water}$$
$$C_3H_8 + 5O_2 \longrightarrow 3CO_2 + 4H_2O$$

The alkenes

Another common family of hydrocarbons found in crude oil is the **alkenes**. In this family there is at least one carbon–carbon double bond. This double bond makes a big difference to the chemistry of the compounds of the family.

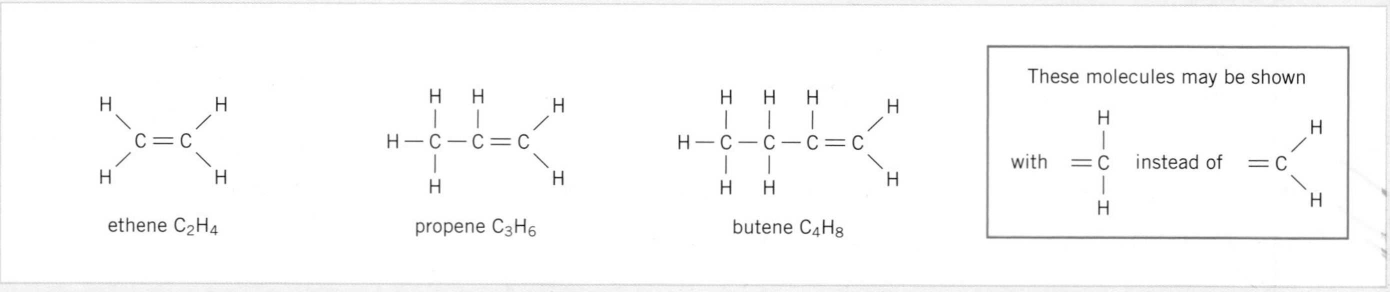

↑ Figure 1: The first four members of the alkane family.

methane CH_4
ethane C_2H_6
propane C_3H_8
butane C_4H_{10}

↓ Figure 2: The combustion reaction of methane with the oxygen in the air provides millions of us with heating, hot water and a way to cook our food.

ethene C_2H_4
propene C_3H_6
butene C_4H_8

These molecules may be shown with =C instead of =C

↑ Figure 3: The first three members of the alkene family.

Useful products from oil

The alkenes, and particularly ethene, are tremendously important in the chemical industry. They are not found in crude oil in very large quantities but are produced by the cracking of the alkanes (see Section 3.3, Example 2).

The alkenes, like all the hydrocarbons, burn in air to form carbon dioxide and water. In oxygen, ethene reacts *explosively* so it is not much good as a fuel!

$$C_2H_4 + 3O_2 \longrightarrow 2CO_2 + 2H_2O$$

The alkenes are also too useful in the chemical industry (for the manufacture of plastics and many other chemicals) to be used as fuels.

Saturated and unsaturated hydrocarbons

Hydrocarbon molecules which have no double bonds in them are called **saturated**. This simply means that there are as many hydrogen atoms as possible in the molecule, and no more can be added. Hydrocarbon molecules with at least one double bond are called **unsaturated** – meaning that more hydrogen atoms *can* be added to these molecules. Unsaturated molecules are much more reactive than saturated ones. This is because the double bond is less than twice as strong as a single bond, making it easier to break one part of the double bond apart than it would be to break a single bond. The result of this is that the alkenes are much more reactive than the alkanes, as the bromine water test shows.

The bromine water test

When bromine is dissolved in water a yellowy-brown liquid known as bromine water results. This is a convenient way to use bromine in the lab.

If the colourless gas ethane, a saturated hydrocarbon, is bubbled through yellow-brown bromine water nothing happens. However, if the colourless gas ethene, an unsaturated hydrocarbon, is bubbled through bromine water the liquid becomes colourless as the bromine reacts with the unsaturated hydrocarbon.

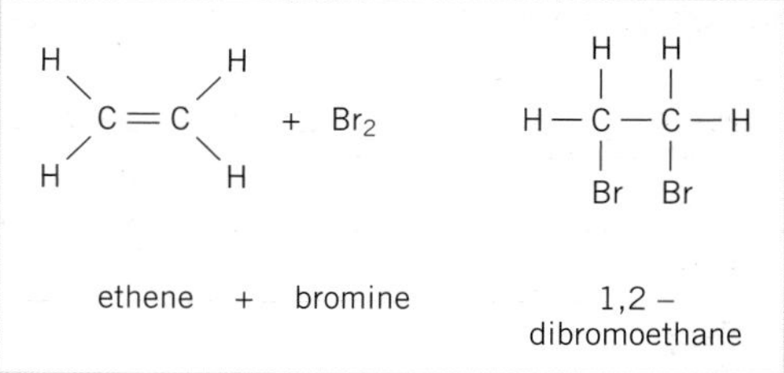

↑ **Figure 4:** The bromine molecule is added to the hydrocarbon across the double bond, forming a saturated compound and removing the bromine (and so the colour) from the bromine water.

? Questions

1 a What is an alkane?

  b Draw the structure of a molecule of pentane.

  c How do alkanes react with oxygen in the air?

  d Give two uses of members of the alkane family.

  e Write a balanced equation showing how butane burns in air.

2 a What is an alkene?

  b Draw the structures of a molecule of pentene.

  c How are the alkenes formed from the alkanes?

  d Give two reasons why the alkenes are not used as fuels.

  e Write a balanced equation showing how butene burns in air.

3 Why is an unsaturated hydrocarbon more reactive than a saturated one?

4 Explain why an alkene but not an alkane turns bromine water colourless.

Key Ideas

⊙ Carbon atoms form the spine of hydrocarbon molecules.

⊙ Hydrocarbons with only single carbon–carbon bonds are known as alkanes.

⊙ Hydrocarbons with at least one carbon–carbon double bond are known as alkenes.

⊙ Alkenes react with bromine water and decolourise it; alkanes do not react.

A polymer is a very large molecule which is made up of long chains of repeating smaller monomer units joined together. A molecule is regarded as a polymer, rather than just a big molecule, when there are at least 50 repeating monomer units in the chain. In some polymers the monomer units are all the same, in others there are a number of different alternating monomer units. The world is full of natural polymers including the proteins, carbohydrates and fats which make up the cells of most living things.

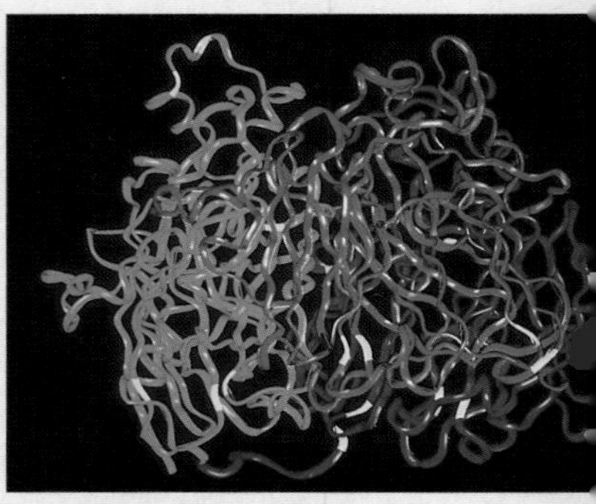

Over the last 50 years or so, we have rapidly developed the ability to make all sorts of synthetic polymers. We can design polymers to have just the properties which make them useful for a particular job. The alkenes and related compounds, with their reactive double bonds, are very important in the manufacture of polymers.

↑ **Figure 1:** Proteins are long chains of monomers known as amino acids. Computer models like this one of Factor VIII (a blood clotting protein) help us imagine what they look like.

Forming polymers

When many small monomer units join together to form a very large polymer, the reaction is known as **polymerisation**. Sometimes the monomers join together and form molecules of water as well, as they join. Often, however, unsaturated monomers join together and no other substance is produced in the reaction. This process is known as **addition polymerisation**.

Unsaturated hydrocarbons contain at least one double bond. This makes them reactive. They are particularly likely to be involved in addition reactions where the double bond opens up and single bonds are formed in its place. This is the type of reaction which takes place when alkenes join together to form a polymer:

$$\text{monomer} + \text{monomer} + \text{monomer} + \ldots \longrightarrow \text{polymer}$$

Making plastics

Plastics are well known artificial polymers. One of the most common and best known plastics is polythene. This is more correctly known as poly(ethene), and it is made by the polymerisation of the simplest alkene, ethene. In the polymerisation reaction the double covalent bonds of the ethene molecules are broken and replaced by single covalent bonds, as hundreds of ethene molecules join together in an addition reaction:

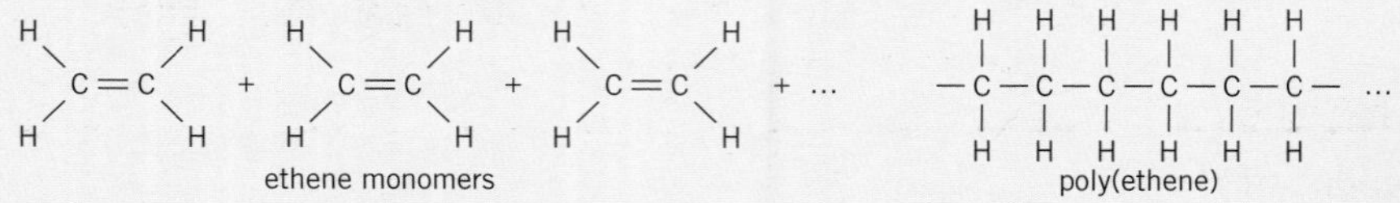

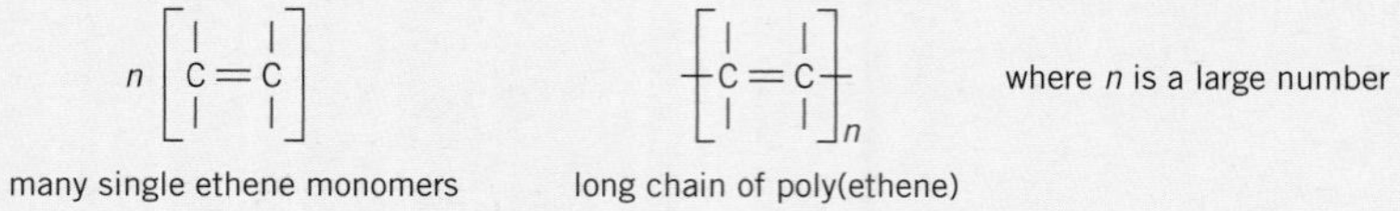

↓ **Figure 2:** Poly(propene) is one important addition polymer. It can be woven into very strong ropes like these, which will not rot or decay, unlike natural alternatives.

ethene monomers   poly(ethene)

This addition polymerisation can be shown in a simpler form:

$$n\begin{bmatrix} \mathrm{C}=\mathrm{C} \end{bmatrix} \qquad \begin{bmatrix} \mathrm{C}=\mathrm{C} \end{bmatrix}_n \qquad \text{where } n \text{ is a large number}$$

many single ethene monomers   long chain of poly(ethene)

Another example of the process of addition polymerisation is in the formation of poly(propene):

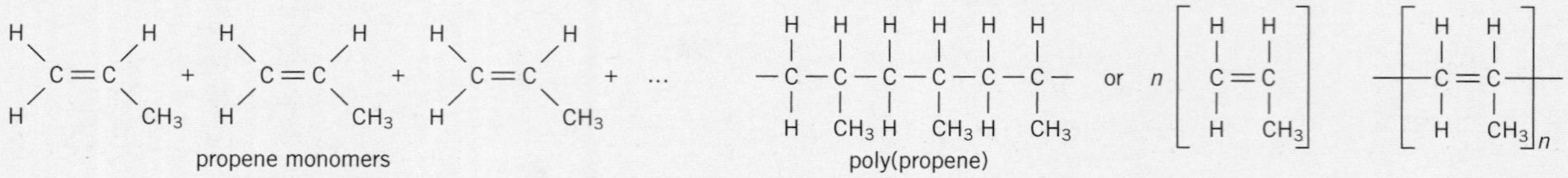

propene monomers   poly(propene)

The iron can be connected to a more reactive metal which will react with oxygen leaving the iron or steel untouched. This is called **sacrificial protection**, because the more reactive metal is 'sacrificed' to protect the iron. The metals most commonly used are zinc and magnesium. A large lump of zinc is often attached to the hulls of steel ships where it is corroded away, needing to be replaced at regular intervals. The iron can also be completely covered by a protective layer of zinc, or **galvanised**. Even if the coating is scratched or damaged, the iron will not corrode because of the sacrificial effect of the zinc.

Another way of preventing iron from corroding is to mix it with other substances to form an alloy which does not corrode. For example, if iron is mixed with chromium it forms a metal known as stainless steel – 'stainless' because it does not rust or corrode. Alloy steels like this are enormously useful. Not only are they immune to corrosion, but the strength and other properties of the metal can be modified to fit them for a wide variety of jobs.

↑ **Figure 3:** Making steel is a hot, noisy business – and can be quite spectacular!

Composition	Steel 1	Steel 2
max % carbon	0.20	0.22
max % sulphur	0.035	0.035

Property	Steel 1	Steel 2
breaking strength (N/mm^2)	410–560	490–630

↑ **Figure 2:** The addition of other elements to iron can change its properties.

? Questions

1 Draw a flow diagram to explain the stages in the extraction of iron in the blast furnace.

2 Tin is an unreactive metal which is used to cover iron and steel.

a Explain how this will prevent the iron from rusting.

b Explain why tin will not be as effective as zinc at protecting the iron, particularly if it gets scratched.

3 Using the data in Figure 2:

a Produce a bar chart to compare the amount of carbon and sulphur in the two steels.

b Explain how

i carbon

ii sulphur

appear to affect the breaking strength of steel.

Key Ideas

⊙ Iron can be extracted from its ore using carbon in a reduction reaction. This is carried out industrially in a blast furnace.

⊙ The solid raw materials used in a blast furnace are iron ore (haematite), coke and limestone.

⊙ Molten iron forms at the bottom of the furnace with molten slag floating on top.

⊙ Iron corrodes easily to form iron oxide or rust. This can be prevented using zinc or magnesium as sacrificial protection or by making alloys with other elements.

4.4 Electrolysis

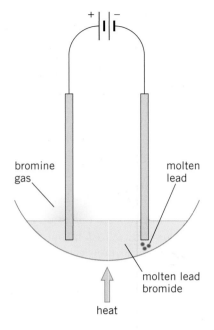

↑ **Figure 2:** Molten lead and brown bromine gas are formed when electricity is passed through molten lead bromide.

The basis of electrolysis is that substances made up of ions can be broken down (decomposed) into simpler substances by passing an electric current through them. The substance being broken down by electrolysis is known as the **electrolyte**.

An electrical circuit is set up with two **electrodes** dipping into the electrolyte. The electrodes are conducting rods, one positive and one negative. They are usually made out of a very inert substance like graphite or platinum so they do not react with either the electrolyte or the products of the reaction. (The positive electrode is sometimes called the *anode* and the negative electrode the *cathode*.)

During electrolysis, positively charged ions move to the negative electrode, and negative ions move to the positive electrode. When the ions reach the electrodes they can lose their charge and be deposited as elements. Depending on the compound being electrolysed gases may be given off or metals deposited at the electrodes.

In the example in Figure 2 the electrical energy has brought about a chemical change – the breakdown of lead bromide into lead and bromine.

$$\text{lead bromide} \longrightarrow \text{lead} + \text{bromine}$$

$$PbBr(l) \longrightarrow Pb(l) + Br_2(g)$$

Lead bromide is an ionic substance. When it is melted the ions are free to move towards the oppositely charged electrode.

Many ionic substances have very high melting points, which makes electrolysis difficult if not impossible. However some dissolve in water – when this happens the ions are once again free to move. The only complication when substances are in solution is that water also forms ions, and so the products at the electrodes are not always easy to predict.

Covalent compounds cannot be split by electrolysis.

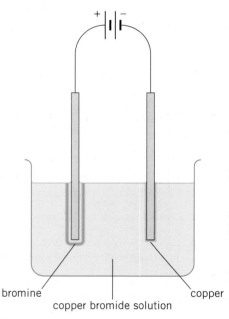

↑ **Figure 3:** When copper bromide is dissolved in water it can be decomposed by electrolysis. The positive copper ions move to the negative electrode and copper metal appears. At the same time the negative bromide ions move to the positive electrode and brown bromine appears:

$$\text{copper bromide} \longrightarrow \text{copper} + \text{bromine}$$

$$CuBr_2(aq) \longrightarrow Cu(s) + Br_2(aq)$$

H What happens at the electrodes?

During electrolysis, ions gain or lose electrons at the electrodes. Electrically neutral atoms or molecules are released. The reactions which take place at the electrodes can be shown by **half equations**. This term is used because what happens at one electrode is only half of the story – you need to know what is happening at both the electrodes to understand the whole reaction.

Example 1: Electrolysis of molten lead bromide

When the positive lead ions move to the negative electrode, they gain electrons in a reduction reaction:

$$Pb^{2+} \ + \ 2e^- \longrightarrow Pb$$

Similarly when the negative bromide ions move to the positive electrode they lose electrons in an oxidation reaction:

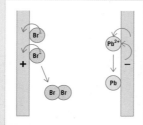

$$2Br^- \ - \ 2e^- \longrightarrow Br_2$$

Sometimes oxidation reactions are written with '$+2e^-$' on the right of the arrow instead of '$-2e^-$' on the left.

In this case the alternative half equation is:

$$2Br^- \longrightarrow Br_2 \ + \ 2e^-$$

Example 2: Electrolysis of copper bromide solution

At the negative electrode there is a reduction reaction:

$$Cu^{2+} \ + \ 2e^- \longrightarrow Cu$$

At the positive electrode there is an oxidation reaction:

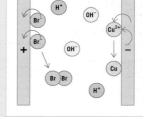

$$2Br^- \ - \ 2e^- \longrightarrow Br_2$$

Notice that a reaction in which electrons are gained is called reduction and one in which electrons are lost is called oxidation, even though oxygen itself may not be involved.

As you can see from these equations, the decomposition of ionic substances during electrolysis involves **redox** reactions, with reduction and oxidation taking place at the same time.

? Questions

1 What is meant by the following terms?

   a electrolysis   **b** electrolyte   **c** electrode

2 Solid ionic substances do not conduct electricity. Why do they conduct electricity if melted or dissolved in water?

3 What happens to ionic compounds as an electric current passes through them?

4 Make a table to show which of these ions would move towards the positive electrode and which towards the negative electrode during electrolysis:

   sodium, iodide, zinc, iron, oxide, aluminium, chloride, fluoride, silver.

   (Use the data at the back of the book to help you.)

5 Draw and label a diagram to show what you would expect to happen if molten sodium chloride was electrolysed.

H 6 Complete and balance the following half equations for reactions at electrodes during electrolysis:

   a $Cl^- \ - \ e^- \longrightarrow Cl_2$

   b $Mg^{2+} + \ ... \longrightarrow Mg$

   c $O^{2-} \ - \ e^- \longrightarrow O_2$

Key Ideas

⊙ Ionic substances which are dissolved in water or melted can be decomposed into simpler substances by passing an electric current through them. This process is called electrolysis.

⊙ Positively charged ions move to the negative electrode and negatively charged electrons move to the positive electrode.

⊙ At the negative electrode positively charged ions gain electrons (reduction). At the positive electrode negatively charged ions lose electrons (oxidation).

⊙ Neutral atoms or molecules are produced by electrolysis.

⊙ The reactions which take place at the electrodes can be represented by balanced half equations.

Using electrolysis

It is impossible to extract reactive metals such as aluminium from their ores using reduction reactions (unless highly reactive metals like sodium are used). Since aluminium oxide is insoluble in water and does not melt below 2000 °C, for years extracting aluminium using electrolysis was also almost impossible. Then in 1886 a 21-year-old American student, Charles Hall, found that if he dissolved aluminium oxide in a substance called cryolite (another aluminium compound) the melting point dropped to 850 °C. This much lower temperature made aluminium extraction by electrolysis a realistic possibility.

The extraction of aluminium

There is more aluminium in the Earth's crust than any other metal, and most of it is in the form of bauxite – aluminium oxide mixed with impurities like sand. The first step in the extraction after the ore has been mined is to purify it, to give white aluminium oxide. This is then dissolved in molten cryolite in special steel tanks lined with carbon (graphite), which acts as the negative electrode. Large positive electrodes, also made of graphite, dip into the tank and an electric current is passed through the mixture. Molten aluminium forms at the negative electrode and is run off and collected. Oxygen forms at the positive electrodes. It immediately reacts with the carbon electrodes to form carbon dioxide, burning them away – so they need frequent replacement.

↑ **Figure 1:** Today, using gold and silver tableware like this is the height of luxury. For many years the extraction of reactive metals like aluminium was terribly difficult, so aluminium was very expensive. In the 19th century only the very rich and privileged could afford to use aluminium plates and cutlery – a far cry from our everyday aluminium drinks cans!

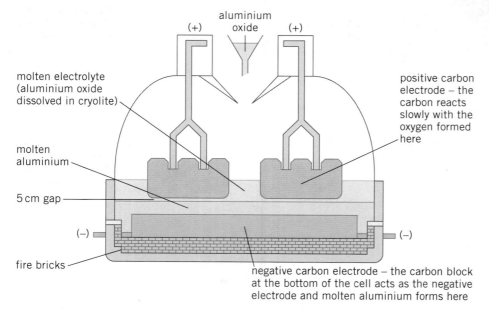

aluminium oxide

(+)　　　　(+)

molten electrolyte (aluminium oxide dissolved in cryolite)

positive carbon electrode – the carbon reacts slowly with the oxygen formed here

molten aluminium

5 cm gap

(–)　　　　(–)

fire bricks

negative carbon electrode – the carbon block at the bottom of the cell acts as the negative electrode and molten aluminium forms here

← **Figure 2:** The extraction of aluminium by electrolysis is still not cheap, as it uses a lot of electricity both for the electrolysis itself and to keep the electrolyte molten.

Why is the extraction of aluminium so important?

Aluminium is a silvery, shiny metal which is surprisingly light – it has a relatively low density for a metal. It is an excellent conductor of heat and electricity and it can be shaped and drawn into wires easily. In addition, although aluminium is a relatively reactive metal, it does not corrode easily. This is because, when aluminium is exposed to air, it immediately reacts with the oxygen in the air to form a thin layer of aluminium oxide (Al_2O_3). This then prevents any further corrosion from taking place, making aluminium more useful than ever.

$$4Al + 3O_2 \longrightarrow 2Al_2O_3$$

Aluminium is not a particularly strong metal when it is pure, but it forms alloys which make it harder, stiffer and stronger so that it makes a good structural material. As a result of all these properties aluminium is an extremely useful metal. It is used for a whole range of goods, from cans, cooking foil and saucepans through to electricity cables, planes and space vehicles.

Purifying metals

Another important use of electrolysis is in purifying metals. For example, when copper is first obtained from its ore it is about 99% pure. The impurities, which include gold, silver and platinum, are enough to affect the ability of copper to conduct electricity, so before it can be used in electric wires it must be purified. A bar of impure copper is used as the positive electrode, and a thin sheet of pure copper is used as the negative electrode. The electrolysis must take place in a solution containing copper ions – usually copper sulphate solution. Copper is lost from the positive electrode – it dissolves – and pure copper is deposited on the negative electrode.

↑ **Figure 3:** Aluminium is present in large amounts in the Earth's crust, and has many different uses. Here it is used in the form of aluminium cladding, covering a sewage treatment plant in Germany.

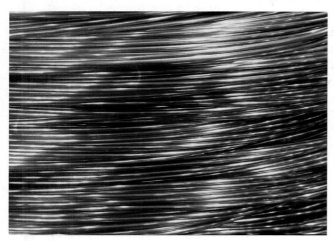

↗ **Figure 4:** To conduct electricity around our homes, copper wires like these are used – so the purification of copper by electrolysis is very important to our everyday lives.

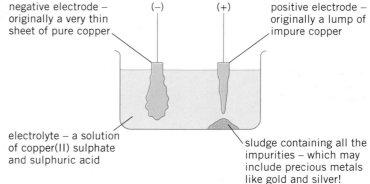

negative electrode – originally a very thin sheet of pure copper

(−) (+)

positive electrode – originally a lump of impure copper

electrolyte – a solution of copper(II) sulphate and sulphuric acid

sludge containing all the impurities – which may include precious metals like gold and silver!

? Questions

1 Make a flow chart to show the extraction of aluminium from its bauxite ore.

2 Why do the positive carbon electrodes used to extract aluminium need regular replacement, whilst the negative carbon electrode does not?

3 Give five different uses of aluminium and for each use suggest which properties of the metal are important.

4 Once tin has been extracted from its ore it is still contaminated by trace elements and needs to be purified further before it can be used to plate steel cans to make 'tin' cans. Suggest how this could be done.

🔑 Key Ideas

⊙ Aluminium is extracted from the ore bauxite by electrolysis.

⊙ Aluminium oxide is dissolved in molten cryolite in a tank with carbon electrodes.

⊙ Molten aluminium is collected at the negative electrode. Oxygen gas is produced which reacts with the positive carbon electrode.

⊙ Copper can be purified by electrolysis with an impure copper positive electrode and a pure copper negative electrode.

More electrolysis

Using electrolysis

The situation when electrolysis is used on a large industrial scale to extract aluminium from its ore or to purify metals like copper can be represented using half equations, as we saw in Section 4.4.

The reactions at the electrodes in the extraction of aluminium from aluminium oxide (Al_2O_3) are represented by the following half equations.

At the negative electrode, positive ions gain electrons:

$$Al^{3+}(l) + 3e^- \longrightarrow Al(l)$$

At the positive electrode, negative ions lose electrons:

$$2O^{2-}(l) - 4e^- \longrightarrow O_2(g)$$

Similarly the events at the electrodes during the purification of copper are as follows.

At the positive electrode impure copper forms copper ions:

$$Cu(s) - 2e^- \longrightarrow Cu^{2+}(aq)$$

At the negative electrode copper ions form copper metal:

$$Cu^{2+}(aq) + 2e^- \longrightarrow Cu(s)$$

Using half equations

Half equations are very important when we want to calculate the amount of substances formed during electrolysis. For example, in the electrolysis of copper bromide solution, the two half equations for the reactions at the electrodes are:

negative electrode: $Cu^{2+}(aq) + 2e^- \longrightarrow Cu(s)$

positive electrode: $2Br^-(aq) - 2e^- \longrightarrow Br_2(aq)$

Notice how the number of electrons produced (lost) by the bromide ions at the positive electrode is the same as the number of electrons needed by the copper ion at the negative electrode – so these half equations are balanced. We can now use the two half equations in calculations involving the amounts of each substance produced at the electrodes. Suppose that 16 g of bromine are produced at the positive electrode when a solution of copper bromide is being electrolysed. We can calculate how much copper is produced at the negative electrode like this:

The A_r of bromine is 80. Bromine molecules have the formula Br_2, so the M_r of bromine is $2 \times 80 = 160$.

The number of moles of bromine molecules produced is $16 / 160 = 0.1$ moles.

The balanced half equations tell us that for every mole of bromine molecules produced, 1 mole of copper atoms is produced, so if 0.1 moles of bromine molecules are produced, 0.1 moles of copper atoms are also produced.

The A_r of copper is 63, so the mass of copper produced is $0.1 \times 63 = 6.3$ g.

↑ **Figure 1:** Thousands of tonnes of aluminium are extracted from bauxite each year – all by the process represented by the half equations shown on the left. The aluminium is often made into sheets and wound onto huge rolls like these.

Sometimes the calculation is a little more difficult. For example, during the production of aluminium, the two half equations involved are:

negative electrode: $Al^{3+}(l) + 3e^- \longrightarrow Al(l)$

positive electrode: $2O^{2-}(l) - 4e^- \longrightarrow O_2(g)$

As it stands these two half equations do not balance – aluminium ions are combining with 3 electrons, while oxygen ions are giving up 4 electrons. For the half equations to balance we must have the same number of electrons in each. To get them to balance in this case we need to multiply the half equation for the negative electrode by 4 and the half equation for the positive electrode by 3:

negative electrode: $4Al^{3+}(l) + 12e^- \longrightarrow 4Al(l)$

positive electrode: $6O^{2-}(l) - 12e^- \longrightarrow 3O_2(g)$

Now the number of electrons produced by the oxide ions at the positive electrode is the same as the number of electrons needed by the aluminium ions at the negative electrode, so we can do the calculation in the same way as before. For example, this is how we calculate the mass of oxygen formed when 5.4 kg of aluminium is produced:

The A_r of aluminium is 27. The mass of aluminium produced is 5.4 kg, which is 5400 g. So the number of moles of aluminium atoms produced is 5400/27 = 200 moles.

The balanced half equations tell us that for every 4 moles of aluminium atoms produced, 3 moles of oxygen molecules are produced, so if 200 moles of aluminium atoms are produced, this will produce $\frac{3}{4} \times 200 = 150$ moles of oxygen molecules.

The A_r of oxygen is 16. Oxygen molecules have the formula O_2, so the M_r of oxygen is 32. This means that the mass of oxygen produced is $150 \times 32 = 4800$ g or 4.8 kg.

- ⊙ If we know the mass/volume of a substance produced at one electrode it is possible to predict the mass/volume of substance which will be produced at the other electrode.

? Questions

1 Complete and balance the following half equations for reactions at electrodes during electrolysis:

 a $Br^- - e^- \longrightarrow Br_2$

 b $Cu^{2+} + ... \longrightarrow Cu$

 c $O^{2-} - e^- \longrightarrow O_2$

2 a Write the half equations for the electrolysis of aluminium oxide.

 b During the electrolysis of aluminium oxide 54 g of molten aluminium is collected at the negative electrode. What volume of oxygen would you expect to be given off at the positive electrode?

3 Electrolysis can be used to coat one metal with another. For example, if a fork is used as the negative electrode with a pure silver positive electrode and the electrolyte contains silver ions (eg silver nitrate solution), silver is plated onto the fork.

 a Produce a diagram to show what is happening during the silver plating of a fork.

 b Give half equations for the events at the electrodes when an object is silver plated.

4.7 Limestone

Metals and their ores are not the only useful substances which can be extracted from the rocks of the Earth. Many other minerals come from the Earth's crust and are used in various ways by people. One of the most important is **limestone**.

What is limestone?

What is the link between the food in your local supermarket, cement and blast furnaces? The answer is limestone! Limestone is a white rock made mainly of calcium carbonate ($CaCO_3$) which has been formed over millions of years from the remains of sea organisms such as corals.

Limestone is quarried around the world on an enormous scale, for use in the chemical industry, in agriculture and in the building industry. Sometimes it is used as it is. Often it is treated and undergoes chemical reactions before it is used.

↑ **Figure 1:** These white cliffs are made of chalk – one type of limestone, formed from the shells of tiny creatures which secreted calcium carbonate.

Uses of limestone

One major use of limestone is as a building material. Throughout Europe many large and famous buildings are made of limestone, although sadly some of them are now showing signs of damage by acid rain – the acid reacts with the calcium carbonate and erodes it away.

When limestone is broken into lumps it is used in the blast furnace in the extraction of iron from its ore, reacting with the impurities in the iron to form slag (see Section 4.3).

Finally, when limestone is powdered it has a number of uses. It can be added to lakes and soils to neutralise acidity. It is often added to lakes where the pH has been lowered due to acid rain.

↑ **Figure 2:** St Paul's cathedral is a famous example of a building made out of limestone blocks.

← **Figure 3:** Glass – made using processed limestone – plays an important role in our lives in many ways. It has many practical uses but it can also be used to create objects of great beauty, as shown here.

Processed limestone

Not only is limestone useful in its pure form, it can also be processed in a number of ways to provide a whole range of valuable products.

← **Figure 4:** This concrete building (The National Theatre) looks very different to St Paul's cathedral – but both are made largely of limestone!

Powdered limestone can be heated to high temperatures with a mixture of sand and sodium carbonate (soda) to make glass. It has been used in this industry for hundreds of years.

In another, very different use, powdered limestone is roasted with powdered clay in a rotary kiln to produce cement, widely used in the building industry. When this cement powder is mixed with water, sand and crushed rock – which may well be limestone too – a slow chemical reaction takes place which produces a hard, stone-like building material called concrete.

When limestone is heated in a furnace (known as a lime kiln), it breaks down to form **quicklime** (calcium oxide) and carbon dioxide in a type of reaction known as **thermal decomposition**.

$$CaCO_3(s) \longrightarrow CaO(s) + CO_2(g)$$

Many other carbonates behave in the same way.

If water is added to quicklime it produces another calcium compound (calcium hydroxide) known as **slaked lime** or **hydrated lime**.

$$CaO(s) + H_2O(l) \longrightarrow Ca(OH)_2(s)$$

Slaked lime is used in agriculture – farmers 'lime' their land, adding slaked lime to improve the fertility and structure of the soil and to balance the pH if the soil is acidic.

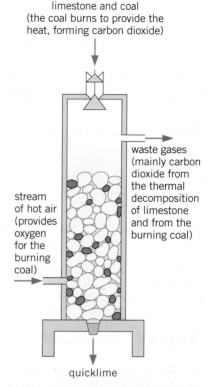

limestone and coal
(the coal burns to provide the heat, forming carbon dioxide)

waste gases
(mainly carbon dioxide from the thermal decomposition of limestone and from the burning coal)

stream of hot air
(provides oxygen for the burning coal)

quicklime

↑ **Figure 5:** Quicklime is produced in a lime kiln. A rotary kiln works in the same way, except that the chemicals are heated in a rotating drum to ensure that they are thoroughly mixed with the stream of hot air.

? Questions

1 Write word equations for:

 a the reaction when limestone is heated in a furnace

 b the reaction when quicklime is reacted with water.

2 Produce a diagram to summarise the different ways in which limestone is used, both as limestone and when processed in various ways.

3 Quicklime is often added to soil and lakes which have been affected by acid rain (often dilute sulphuric acid).

 a Why is quicklime added?

 b Give a word equation for the reaction which occurs.

 c Write a balanced chemical equation for the reaction between quicklime and sulphuric acid.

H **4** Both quicklime and slaked lime are used to control soil pH.

 a Work out the equations for the reaction between quicklime and sulphuric acid and for slaked lime and sulphuric acid.

 b If 56 g of quicklime are needed to neutralise a particular area of soil, how much slaked lime would be needed to do the same job?

🔑 Key Ideas

⊙ Limestone is calcium carbonate.

⊙ Limestone is quarried and used in a variety of ways, both as limestone and as a number of derivatives.

⊙ Heating limestone gives quicklime and adding water to quicklime forms slaked lime.

⊙ The main uses of limestone and its derivatives are in the building industry, in agriculture and in glass making.

Plants are vital for life on Earth. To grow successfully plants need nitrogen to form proteins, yet they cannot use nitrogen from the air. Although nitrogen gas makes up around 80% of the air around us it is very unreactive and inert, so plants cannot use it. Instead, plants take in soluble nitrates through their roots. These nitrates are then returned to the soil when the plants rot and die.

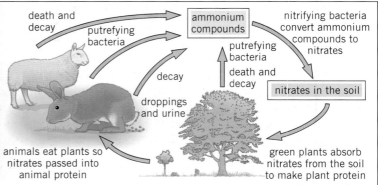

↖ **Figure 1:** Plants grow surrounded by nitrogen in the air. They need it and yet they cannot use it – they have to rely on nitrates from the soil to supply their needs.

When people harvest plants for food, the nitrates in those plants are not returned to the soil and need to be replaced in some other way to keep the soil fertile. Today this is usually done by using fertilisers which contain nitrates. These were made possible by a process developed by a young German chemist called Fritz Haber at the beginning of the 20th century.

What is the Haber process?

The Haber process provides us with a way of turning the nitrogen in the air into ammonia, a compound with a number of uses. The raw materials are nitrogen from the air and hydrogen obtained from natural gas (methane). The purified gases are passed over an iron catalyst at high temperatures (about 450 °C) and pressures (about 200 atmospheres). The product of the reaction is ammonia. However, this reaction is reversible, which means that the ammonia breaks down again into hydrogen and nitrogen. To reduce this, the ammonia is cooled, liquefied and removed as soon as it is formed. Any hydrogen and nitrogen left is recycled and reacted again.

nitrogen + hydrogen $\rightleftharpoons$ ammonia

$$N_2(g) + 3H_2(g) \underset{\text{iron catalyst}}{\overset{450\,°C,\ 200\ atm}{\rightleftharpoons}} 2NH_3(g)$$

The reaction conditions for the Haber process are chosen to give a reasonable yield of ammonia as quickly as possible.

The economics of the Haber process

The industrial version of the Haber process is a compromise designed to make ammonia as rapidly and cheaply as possible. In any manufacturing process the costs must be kept as low as possible to maximise profit when the product is sold. For example, the catalyst which Haber used when he first worked on his process in the laboratory was too expensive, so a cheaper iron catalyst was used for the industrial process.

There are two different factors to consider – the yield of ammonia and the rate of reaction – both of which depend on the reaction conditions. If the reacting temperature is lower, more ammonia is formed in the reacting mixture, but very slowly. Increasing the temperature means that the reaction happens more quickly, but the yield of ammonia is reduced. If the pressure is higher more ammonia is formed in the mixture, but it would be incredibly expensive to build a factory to withstand such very high pressures. The practical solution is to use moderate temperatures and pressures.

Section 9.6 includes more detail on the factors affecting the production of ammonia.

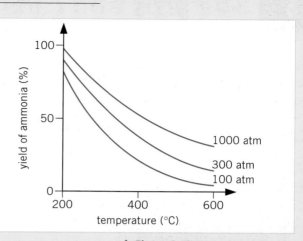

↑ **Figure 2:** The graph shows the effect of different temperatures and pressures on the yield of ammonia in the Haber process.

? Questions

1 a Why is nitrogen so important?

b Explain why plants and animals cannot simply make use of nitrogen from the air.

c Explain how nitrogen is moved around in a natural cycle through living organisms.

2 a Draw a flow diagram to show the events of the Haber process.

b Why is the Haber process so important to us?

H **3 a** What is the effect on the yield of ammonia if the Haber process operates at:

  i 200 atm and 350 °C

  ii 400 atm and 450 °C

  iii 200atm and 450 °C?

b Explain how these different conditions affect the rate of the reaction in the Haber process and suggest why the operating conditions were chosen.

🔑 Key Ideas

- ⊙ Air is almost 80% nitrogen.
- ⊙ Ammonia is manufactured in the Haber process from nitrogen in the air and hydrogen from methane gas.
- ⊙ The conditions of the Haber process are designed to get a reasonable yield of ammonia as rapidly and cheaply as possible.

Much of the ammonia formed from nitrogen by the Haber process is used in further chemical reactions. The main one is the oxidation of ammonia to form nitric acid.

Using ammonia

First, ammonia gas reacts with oxygen in the air in the presence of a hot platinum catalyst. This forms nitrogen monoxide, a colourless gas:

ammonia + oxygen $\longrightarrow$ nitrogen monoxide + water

$4NH_3(g) + 5O_2(g) \longrightarrow 4NO(g) + 6H_2O(g)$

The nitrogen monoxide gas is cooled and then reacted with more oxygen and water to form nitric acid solution:

$6NO(g) + 3O_2(g) + 2H_2O(l) \longrightarrow 4HNO_3(aq) + 2NO(g)$

The nitric acid produced can then be used in a variety of ways. About 75% is used to make nitrate fertilisers, where the nitric acid is often reacted with more ammonia in a neutralisation reaction to form ammonium nitrate. Another 15% of the nitric acid produced is used to make explosives and the remaining 10% is used in a variety of other manufacturing processes.

 Science people

The story of Fritz Haber

Fritz Haber was born in the German town of Breslau in 1868. He became a research chemist and lecturer at the technical college in Karlsruhe. As part of his work in 1908 he discovered a way of combining hydrogen and nitrogen to form ammonia.

By this time Germany was already preparing for the war which would become the First World War. The military leaders realised that once war was declared Germany would be blockaded. This in turn meant that they would need to be self-sufficient in many things, including food and weapons. To grow enough food meant lots of fertiliser, and weapons need explosives.

To make nitrate fertiliser and explosives requires nitric acid, easily made from ammonia. Fritz Haber's simple process was the answer, and he sold it to a major German chemical company. Carl Bosch, a brilliant chemical engineer, then designed a chemical plant which could manufacture ammonia using Haber's process.

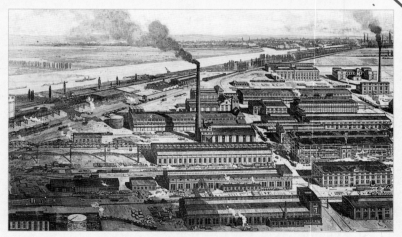

↑ **Figure 1** The thousands of tonnes of ammonia produced in this factory allowed the Germans to feed themselves and make new weapons throughout the First World War.

Haber's process may have prolonged the war, resulting in the loss of hundreds of thousands of lives on all sides. However, since the end of the war, the Haber process has been responsible for the manufacture of millions of tonnes of nitrate fertiliser which improves crop yields and feeds hungry people. Although manufacture of explosives has also continued, far more fertiliser has been made than explosives.

Using nitrogen-based fertilisers

Adding relatively cheap nitrogen-based fertilisers to the soil has been a great advantage to the human race in many ways. In the developed world it has made possible cheap and readily available food for everyone, while in the developing world it is helping to supply more food where it is desperately needed.

However, there are some problems which go with the use of these fertilisers, particularly in the developed world where they are very heavily used. The nitrates from the fertilisers get carried by rainwater into streams, rivers, lakes and groundwater. Once in the waterways they can have two damaging effects. They can cause excess plant growth in the water. When this dies and decays it uses up all the oxygen so that fish and other animals can no longer survive. This is called **eutrophication**.

↑ **Figure 2:** Nitrogen-based fertilisers have brought us great benefits – but everything has a price… .

The nitrate ions also get into the drinking water supply, causing problems for babies and young children. The pollution affects the blood so it does not carry oxygen properly. Small babies can turn blue and even die as a result.

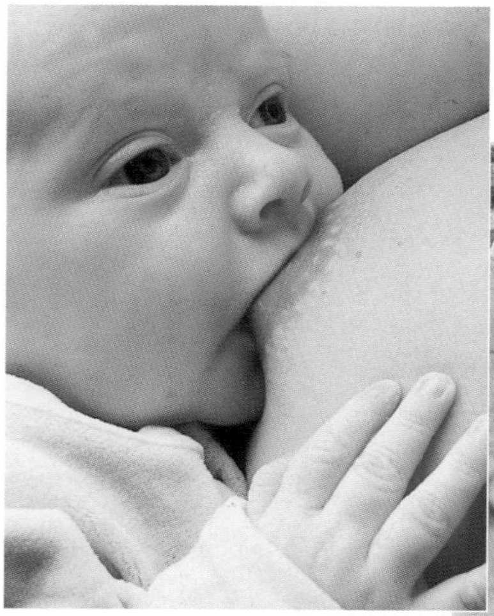

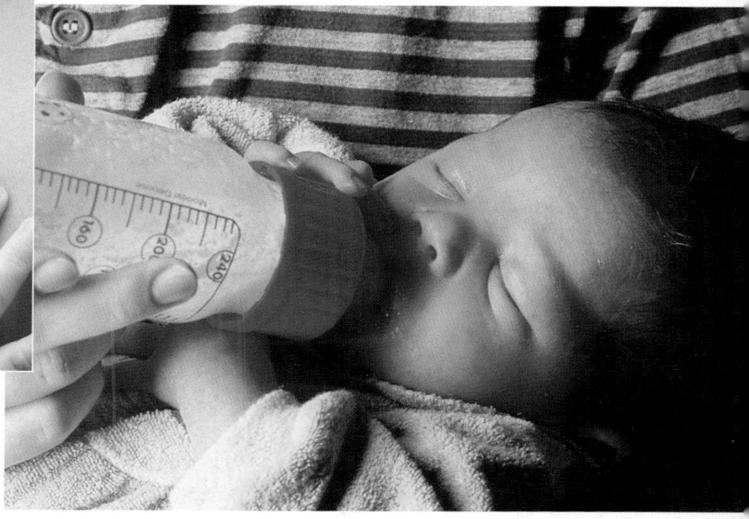

→ **Figure 3:** Bottle-fed babies are most at risk from nitrate pollution as the ions are in the water they are drinking. But even breast-fed babies are not completely safe, as the effects of nitrate ion pollution can reach them through their mother's milk.

Questions

1 a How is nitrogen-based fertiliser made from ammonia?

  H b Give a balanced equation for the reaction between ammonia and nitric acid.

2 a The First World War accelerated the industrial application of the Haber process. How?

  b Do you think Fritz Haber should have kept his discovery to himself? Give your arguments one way or the other.

3 Imagine that some people are trying to ban the use of nitrate fertilisers on farms in your area. Farmers and others are angry. People are getting very heated on both sides. Produce a leaflet which gives a balanced view of the issues, explaining the benefits and the risks of nitrate fertilisers. Try to devise a solution to the problem which would be acceptable to both sides.

Key Ideas

- Nitrogen can be used to manufacture several important chemicals, including nitrogen-based fertilisers.

- Ammonia can be oxidised to form nitric acid which is used to make nitrogen-based fertilisers and explosives.

- Nitrates can cause problems if they find their way into streams, rivers or groundwater and contaminate drinking water.

1 Limestone is an important raw material.

a Limestone has many uses. Choose from the list **two** important materials made from limestone.

> cement   diesel oil   glass
> poly(ethene)   sodium hydroxide
> sulphuric acid   (2 marks)

b The diagram shows a lime kiln. The limestone is heated by the burning coal.

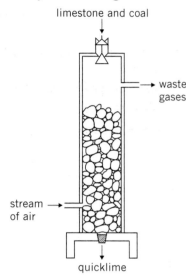

limestone and coal

→ waste gases

stream → of air

quicklime

i Suggest why hot air is blown into the lime kiln.   (1 mark)

ii Give two reactions which produce carbon dioxide in the lime kiln.   (2 marks)

c i Quicklime (calcium oxide) can be converted to slaked lime (calcium hydroxide) by adding water.

Write a word equation to represent this reaction.

> ...... + ... ⟶ ......   (1 mark)

ii Why do farmers sometimes add slaked lime to acidic soil?   (1 mark)

(Total 7 marks)
AQA specimen question

2 Ammonium nitrate is used as a fertiliser.

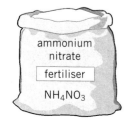

ammonium nitrate

fertiliser

NH_4NO_3

a i How many different elements are there in ammonium nitrate?   (1 mark)

ii For its use as a fertiliser, which is the most important element in ammonium nitrate?   (1 mark)

iii Give **one** reason why fertilisers are added to soil.   (1 mark)

b Ammonia, NH_3, is also used as a fertiliser. Ammonia is made from the raw materials air, natural gas and water.

i Which raw material contains nitrogen?   (1 mark)

ii Copy and complete the word equation for the formation of ammonia from its elements:

> nitrogen + ... ⇌ ammonia   (1 mark)

iii What is meant by ⇌ in the word equation?   (1 mark)

(Total 6 marks)
AQA specimen question

3 a Iron can be extracted from iron oxide in a blast furnace.

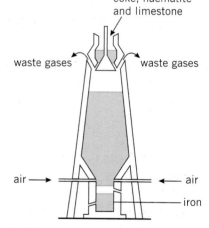

coke, haematite and limestone

waste gases   waste gases

air →   ← air

← iron

i Which **one** of the substances added to the furnace contains the iron oxide?   (1 mark)

ii Inside the furnace the coke (carbon) burns in air to release heat. Name the type of reaction that transfers heat to the surroundings.   (1 mark)

b Carbon monoxide is formed in the furnace. The carbon monoxide reacts with iron oxide to make iron.

Balance the chemical equation for this reaction:

> Fe_2O_3 + ... CO ⟶ ... Fe + ... CO_2
(1 mark)

c To gain full marks you should write down your ideas in good English. Put them into a sensible order and use the correct scientific words.

Aluminium can be extracted from a mineral called bauxite.

  i Bauxite contains aluminium oxide. Describe how aluminium is extracted from aluminium oxide. (3 marks)

  ii About five thousand years passed between the first extraction of iron and that of aluminium. Explain why. (2 marks)

(Total 8 marks)

AQA specimen question

4 Electrolysis is an important process. During electrolysis, substances made of ions (the electrolyte) can be broken down onto simpler substances by passing an electric current through them. Electrolysis is sometimes used to extract metals from their ores.

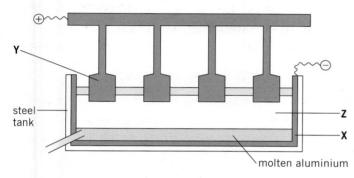

a The diagram shows the apparatus used to extract aluminium metal from its ore, aluminium oxide.

  i What are the parts labelled **X**, **Y** and **Z**? (3 marks)

  ii What is happening at part **X**? (1 mark)

  iii Why does part **Y** have to be replaced regularly? (2 marks)

b Although aluminium is one of the most common metals in the Earth's crust, it has only been extracted easily in useful quantities for a hundred years or so. Why did it take so long before aluminium could be extracted successfully? (3 marks)

c Electrolysis can only be used with ionic substances, and then only when they are either molten or in solution in water. Why is this? (2 marks)

d Give **one** other use of electrolysis in addition to the extraction of metals. (1 mark)

(Total 12 marks)

H 5 Electrolysis can be used in purifying copper, as seen in the diagram.

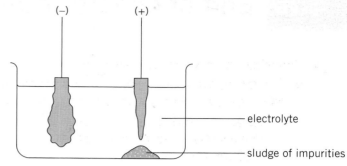

a What is the most commonly used electrolyte in this reaction? (1 mark)

b Explain in words what is happening at the positive electrode. (2 marks)

c Explain in words what is happening at the negative electrode. (2 marks)

d Give half equations for the reactions at:

  i the positive electrode (2 marks)

  ii the negative electrode. (2 marks)

(Total 9 marks)

5.1 The history of the atmosphere

Scientists think that the Earth was formed about 4.5 billion years ago. To begin with it was a molten ball of rock and minerals and for its first billion years it was a very violent place.

The Earth's surface was covered with volcanoes belching fire and smoke into the atmosphere.

The volcanoes released nitrogen and carbon dioxide gas, which formed the early atmosphere, along with water vapour, which condensed as it rose into cooler air and fell as rain to form the first oceans. Comets also brought water to the Earth – as icy comets rained down on the surface of the Earth they melted, adding to the water supplies. Even today many thousands of tonnes of water fall onto the surface of the Earth from space every year.

So as the Earth began to stabilise, the early atmosphere was probably mainly carbon dioxide, with some nitrogen and water vapour and traces of methane and ammonia – in other words, very like the atmospheres which we know exist today on the planets Mars and Venus.

↑ **Figure 1:** Volcanoes moved chemicals from within the Earth to the surface and into the newly forming atmosphere.

← **Figure 2:** The surface of one of Jupiter's moons called Io, with its small atmosphere and active volcanoes. This photograph probably gives us a reasonable glimpse of what our own Earth was like billions of years ago.

Q Ideas and Evidence

How do we know what the atmosphere of the early Earth was like? Of course we cannot know for sure! However chemists have reconstructed what they think the atmosphere must have been like, based on evidence from gas bubbles trapped in rocks and from the atmospheres of other planets in the solar system.

The effect of life

After the initial violent years of the history of the Earth the atmosphere remained relatively stable – until life first appeared on Earth. The scientific view is that life on Earth began some 3.4 billion years ago, in the form of simple bacteria-like organisms which could make food for themselves using the breakdown of other chemicals as a source of energy. Later, bacteria and other simple organisms such as algae evolved which could use the energy of the sun to make their own food in the process of photosynthesis with oxygen as a waste product.

By 2 billion years ago the levels of oxygen were rising steadily as algae and bacteria filled the seas, all photosynthesising. More and more plants of increasing complexity evolved, all of them also carrying out photosynthesis and making oxygen:

carbon dioxide + water + [energy from the sun] $\longrightarrow$ sugar + oxygen

When plants had evolved and successfully colonised most of the surface of the Earth, the atmosphere became increasingly rich in oxygen. Conditions were now favourable for the evolution of animals – organisms which could not make their own food and needed oxygen to respire. On the other hand, many of the earliest living microorganisms could not tolerate oxygen (because they had evolved without it) and they largely died out as there were fewer and fewer places where they could live.

↑ **Figure 3:** Some of the first photosynthesising bacteria probably lived in colonies, like these stromatolites. They grew in water and released oxygen into the early atmosphere.

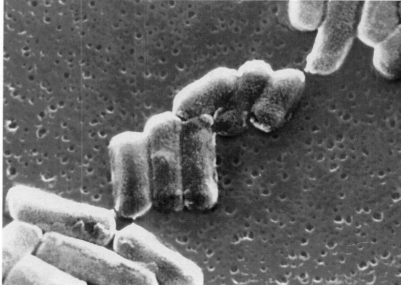

→ **Figure 4:** Bacteria such as these *Clostridium perfringens* not only *do not need* oxygen – they *die* if they are exposed to it. But in decaying tissue and in marshy rotting soil they still survive and breed.

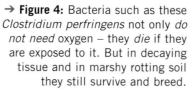

? Questions

1 **a** How was the atmosphere of the early Earth formed?

b What were the main gases it contained?

2 Why was there no life on Earth for several billion years?

3 How have we developed our current picture of the early development of the Earth and its atmosphere?

O—n Key Ideas

⊙ The first billion years of the Earth's existence was marked by intense volcanic activity.

⊙ This released the gases which formed the early atmosphere and water vapour which condensed to form the oceans.

⊙ As plants colonised the Earth there was more oxygen – and fewer microorganisms which could not tolerate oxygen.

What happened to the atmosphere?

We think that the early atmosphere of the Earth contained a great deal of carbon dioxide, yet the modern atmosphere of the Earth has only around 0.04% of this gas. Where has it all gone? The answer is mostly into living organisms and into the materials which are derived from living organisms.

Carbon dioxide is taken up by plants and turned into new plant material during photosynthesis. Then animals eat the plants and the carbon is transferred to the animal tissues, including bones, teeth and shells. Over millions of years ago the dead bodies of huge numbers of these living organisms accumulated at the bottom of vast oceans where they formed sedimentary carbonate rocks like limestone. Some were crushed by movements of the Earth and heated within the crust and they formed fossil fuels such as coal and oil. In this way much of the carbon dioxide from the ancient atmosphere became locked up within the Earth's crust.

Carbon dioxide also dissolved in the oceans, forming insoluble carbonate compounds which fell to the bottom and helped to form carbonate rocks.

At the same time, the small amounts of ammonia and methane remaining in the atmosphere reacted with the oxygen formed by the plants. The oxygen removed these poisonous gases and the levels of nitrogen and carbon dioxide increased.

$$CH_4 + 2O_2 \longrightarrow CO_2 + 2H_2O$$

$$4NH_3 + 3O_2 \longrightarrow 2N_2 + 6H_2O$$

By 200 million years ago the proportions of the different gases in the atmosphere of the Earth were very much the same as they are now (see Figure 3).

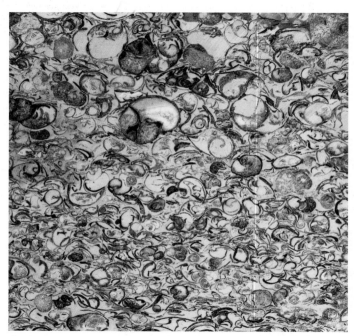

↑ **Figure 1:** Carbonate rocks contain clear evidence of organisms which lived millions of years ago. This piece of Bethersden Marble contains specimens of *Viviparus elongatus* that lived in the Cretaceous period. Along with the dinosaurs, they are now preserved with their ancient carbon in the structure of our rocks.

H   The nitrogen gas in the atmosphere came partly from the reaction between ammonia and oxygen (above). But the main source of nitrogen in the air was the action of bacteria on the cells of dead and decaying plants and animals. The nitrogen-containing compounds (mainly proteins) in the bodies of plants and animals are broken down and nitrogen is released into the air. The bacteria bringing about this release of nitrogen are known as **denitrifying bacteria**.

The oxygen released into the atmosphere by plants was vital for the development of animal life. It also resulted in the formation of an ozone layer in the upper atmosphere (ozone is three oxygen atoms joined together, O_3). This was another important step in the evolution of life on Earth, because the ozone layer filters out some of the harmful ultraviolet radiation from the sun. The presence of the ozone layer made it possible for a much wider variety of new living organisms to evolve, because they did not need to be able to withstand so much ultraviolet radiation. ↓

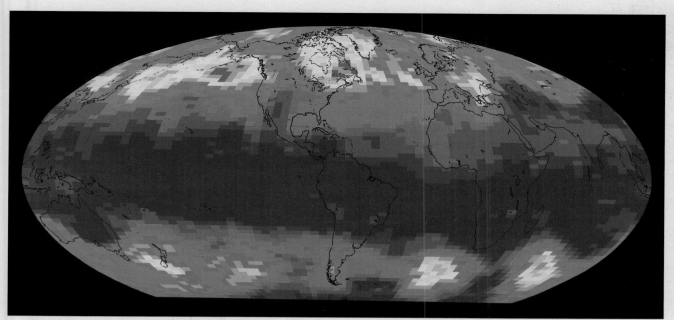

↑ **Figure 2:** This computer-enhanced image shows how the thickness of the ozone layer varies around the Earth. The ozone layer still protects the Earth from harmful ultraviolet radiation, although human activities are damaging it and reducing the protection it gives.

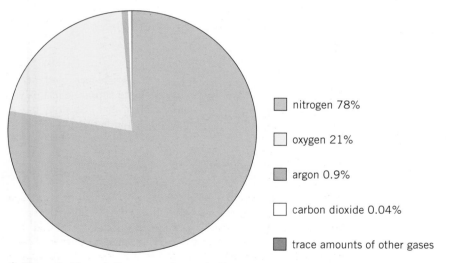

- nitrogen 78%
- oxygen 21%
- argon 0.9%
- carbon dioxide 0.04%
- trace amounts of other gases

↑ **Figure 3:** The relative proportions of nitrogen, oxygen and other gases in the atmosphere.

? Questions

1 What are the main gases which make up the atmosphere of the Earth?

2 How has the carbon dioxide which we think made up a large proportion of the early atmosphere of the Earth become a substantial part of the modern Earth's crust?

H 3 Explain the role of living organisms in determining the proportions of nitrogen, oxygen and ozone in the modern atmosphere.

⊙━ Key Ideas

- ⊙ Most of the carbon from the carbon dioxide in the air became locked up in fossil fuels and sedimentary rocks like carbonates.

- ⊙ Methane and ammonia in the air reacted with the oxygen.

- ⊙ For 200 million years the proportions of the different gases in the atmosphere have stayed stable.

H
- ⊙ Nitrogen gas was also released into the air by the action of denitrifying bacteria.

- ⊙ The ozone layer formed from oxygen and protects against ultraviolet radiation.

The carbon cycle

Over thousands of years, the levels of carbon dioxide in the atmosphere have probably remained fairly stable due to the natural carbon cycle, in which carbon moves between oceans, rocks and atmosphere.

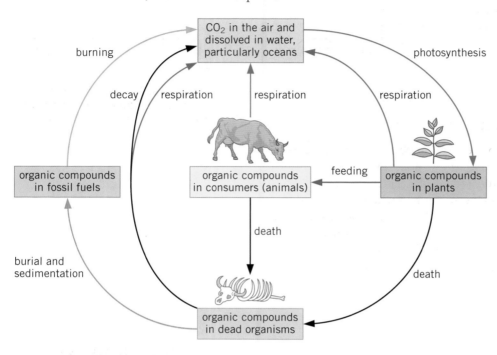

← **Figure 1:** The carbon cycle in nature has maintained the atmospheric level of carbon dioxide for 200 million years.

Left to itself, the carbon cycle is self-regulating. The oceans act as massive reservoirs of carbon dioxide, absorbing excess when it is produced and releasing it when it is in short supply. Plants also soak up excess carbon dioxide from the atmosphere. The plants and oceans are often called carbon dioxide **sinks**.

Carbon dioxide moves back into the atmosphere from the respiration of living things and also from volcanoes. Carbonate rocks are sometimes moved deep into the Earth by geological activity – the movements of the Earth's crust. If that rock then becomes involved in volcanic activity, the heat causes the breakdown of the carbonates and the release of carbon dioxide gas as the volcano erupts.

↓ **Figure 2:** We rely more and more on electricity to support our lifestyles – and much of that electricity is produced by the burning of fossil fuels, which releases carbon dioxide into the atmosphere.

The changing balance

Over the last 50 or so years people have increased the amount of carbon dioxide released into the atmosphere tremendously. Burning fossil fuels to produce electricity, heat homes and power cars has enormously increased carbon dioxide production.

There is no doubt that the levels of carbon dioxide in the atmosphere are increasing. The data shown in Figure 3 were collected from a mountain top in Hawaii. The annual fluctuations in the levels of carbon dioxide are due to seasonal differences in plants and show how important plants are for 'fixing' carbon dioxide and removing it from the atmosphere. The overall trend for the 30 years has been relentlessly upwards.

The balance between the carbon dioxide produced and the carbon dioxide which can be absorbed by carbon dioxide sinks is a very important one to maintain. When fossil fuels are burned, carbon which was locked up hundreds of millions of years ago in the bodies of living animals is released as carbon dioxide into the atmosphere. For example:

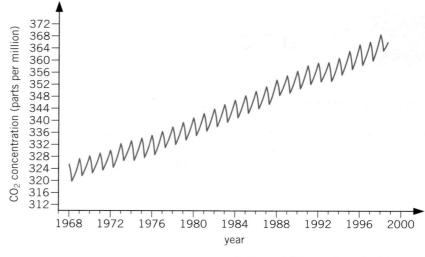

↑ **Figure 3:** The carbon dioxide levels in the atmosphere have been steadily climbing for many years.

propane + oxygen $\longrightarrow$ carbon dioxide + water

$$C_3H_8 + 5O_2 \longrightarrow 3CO_2 + 4H_2O$$

As the carbon dioxide levels go up, so the reaction between carbon dioxide and sea water increases, resulting in the formation of insoluble carbonates (mainly calcium carbonate) which are deposited as sediment on the bottom of the ocean and soluble hydrogencarbonates (mainly calcium and magnesium) which simply remain in solution in the sea water. In this way the seas and oceans act as a buffer, absorbing excess carbon dioxide but releasing it if necessary. However, this buffering system cannot cope quickly enough to deal with all the additional carbon dioxide currently being poured out into the atmosphere.

? Questions

1 a How does carbon dioxide move into and out of the atmosphere?

  b What has caused the current increase in the levels of carbon dioxide in the atmosphere?

2 Use the data in Figure 3 to answer these questions.

  a What was the approximate concentration of carbon dioxide in the atmosphere in 1984?

  b By how much did the level of carbon dioxide in the atmosphere increase between 1968 and the year 2000?

  c Express your answer to part **b** as a percentage of the carbon dioxide concentration in the year 1968.

  d Produce a bar chart to show the carbon dioxide levels in the years 1970, 1980, 1990 and 2000.

3 a Explain how the seas and oceans normally act as a buffer when extra carbon dioxide is produced.

  b What has happened in the last 50 years or so which means that the ocean carbon dioxide sinks can no longer cope?

0—⊓ Key Ideas

⊙ Levels of gases such as carbon dioxide have been largely self-regulating.

⊙ In recent years levels of carbon dioxide have increased as a result of the excess burning of fossil fuels.

⊙ Carbonate rocks may release carbon dioxide through volcanic activity.

⊙ The burning of fossil fuels is increasing the level of carbon dioxide in the atmosphere beyond the ability of the oceans to absorb the excess.

The rocks which make up the Earth's crust hold many clues to the history of the Earth. They have fossils which help us build up a picture of the evolution of life on Earth, they contain radioactive elements which enable us to estimate the age of the Earth itself, and within the patterns of the rocks and the gases contained in them is the story of the way the Earth has formed and changed over the millennia.

The three main types of rock are:

- ⊙ **igneous** – formed from molten magma (eg *quartz*, *granite*, and *basalt*)

- ⊙ **metamorphic** – formed from other rocks by the extremely high temperatures and pressures under the surface of the Earth (eg *marble* from limestone, *slate* from shale)

- ⊙ **sedimentary** – formed when fossils and the weathered fragments of other rocks are deposited in layers, usually under the sea (eg *limestone*, *sandstone* and *shale*).

These three different types of rock continually change from one type to another in a slow cycle lasting millions of years – a process known as the *rock cycle*.

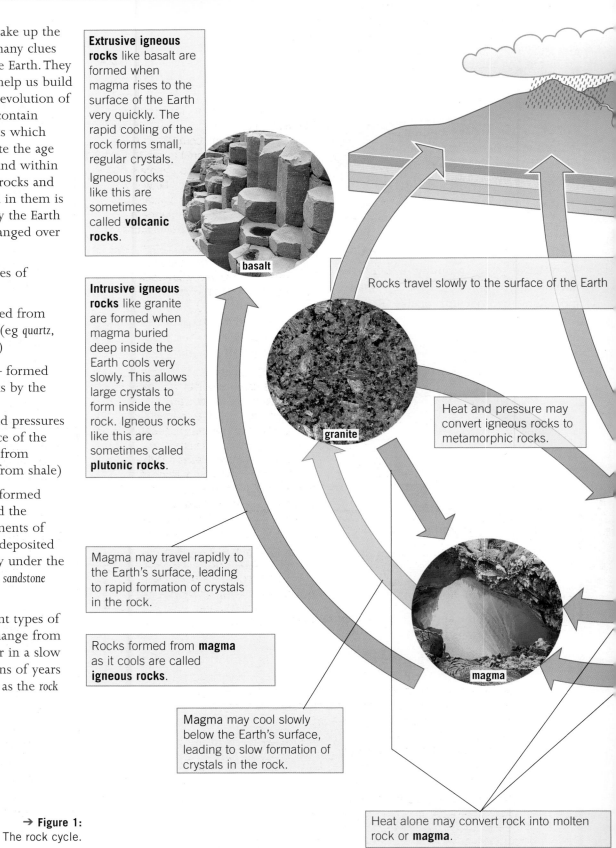

Extrusive igneous rocks like basalt are formed when magma rises to the surface of the Earth very quickly. The rapid cooling of the rock forms small, regular crystals.

Igneous rocks like this are sometimes called **volcanic rocks**.

basalt

Intrusive igneous rocks like granite are formed when magma buried deep inside the Earth cools very slowly. This allows large crystals to form inside the rock. Igneous rocks like this are sometimes called **plutonic rocks**.

Rocks travel slowly to the surface of the Earth

granite

Heat and pressure may convert igneous rocks to metamorphic rocks.

Magma may travel rapidly to the Earth's surface, leading to rapid formation of crystals in the rock.

Rocks formed from **magma** as it cools are called **igneous rocks**.

magma

Magma may cool slowly below the Earth's surface, leading to slow formation of crystals in the rock.

Heat alone may convert rock into molten rock or **magma**.

→ **Figure 1:**
The rock cycle.

Rocks are subject to **weathering** and **erosion** at the Earth's surface. These processes break the rock up into tiny pieces which are transported as sediments by rivers. Eventually the sediments end up in the Earth's oceans and lakes.

As layers of sediment are submerged beneath more and more layers above them, they become compacted due to the weight of material above them. Water carrying dissolved minerals may seep into the spaces between the layers. The minerals crystallise between the layers, holding them together. This is called **cementation**.

As a result of burial and cementation, the layers of sediment become converted into **sedimentary rock** – a process called **lithification**.

in a process called **uplift**.

sandstone

Sedimentary rocks include shale, sandstone, mudstone and limestone. Often the sediment is tiny bits of broken rocks, such as the silica which makes up sandstone. In other cases it is the shells of millions upon millions of living creatures from early seas which make up limestone. Clearly defined layers in a sedimentary rock show that the deposition was discontinuous – there was a break in the laying down of the material. Some sedimentary deposits even show ripple marks or wave patterns in the rock, showing how the original sediments were deposited by water.

marble

When **sedimentary rocks** are subjected to high temperatures and pressures they are turned into **metamorphic rocks**. Different temperatures and pressures cause different changes in the crystal structures inside the rock. For example, at relatively low temperatures shale becomes slate, while at higher temperatures it may become schist or gneiss.

Marble is a very common metamorphic rock, produced from limestone. It is used in many buildings, and for statues.

Key Ideas

- There are three main types of rock – igneous, metamorphic and sedimentary.

- These three types of rock slowly change from one type to another in a process called the rock cycle.

- Sedimentary rocks contain evidence of how they were deposited.

Questions

1 Produce a table to show the main types of rocks, how they are formed, and examples of each type.

2 a What is the difference between extrusive and intrusive igneous rock?

  b What conditions are needed to form metamorphic rocks?

  c What is magma?

3 Summarise the rock cycle in a flow chart, starting with the weathering of rocks at the Earth's surface and finishing with the formation of two types of igneous rock.

It may seem that the crust of the Earth is solid and unmoving, but below its surface the Earth teems with restless activity causing great areas of the crust, known as **tectonic plates**, to constantly move across the surface.

Ideas and Evidence

According to the theory of plate tectonics, the continents of the Earth were once joined together as one land mass. Figure 1 shows the vast 'supercontinent' of Pangaea which is believed to have existed up until about 200 million years ago. Slowly Pangaea split in two, forming the northern continent of Laurasia and the southern continent of Gondwanaland by about 160 million years ago. The land masses continued to move apart and about 100 million years ago they began to resemble the map of the world we know today. Evidence for these ideas comes from the similarity of the fossils and rock structures found on the east coast of South America and the west coast of Africa.

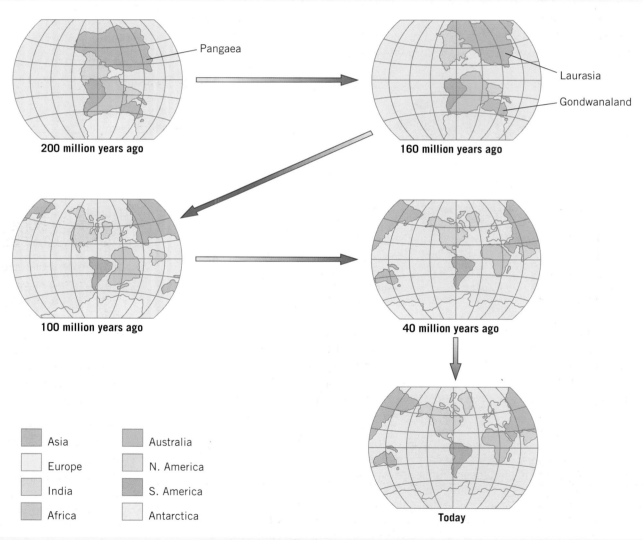

↑ Figure 1: The break-up of Pangaea into Laurasia and Gondwanaland led eventually to the formation of the land masses we recognise today. Notice how, 100 million years ago, India was still moving rapidly northwards to take up the position it occupies today. The collision between India and the continent of Asia produced the mountain range we call the Himalayas.

Movements of the tectonic plates are very slow – only a few centimetres a year – but they are unbelievably powerful. They are caused by radioactive decay deep within the Earth which produces vast amounts of energy. This energy heats up magma (molten rock) which expands, becomes less dense and rises towards the surface, being replaced by cooler material. It is these *convection currents* which push the tectonic plates over the surface of the Earth. The slow but large-scale movements of the tectonic plates have caused mountain ranges to be formed over millions of years and ancient mountain belts to disappear – we only know they existed because of the tell-tale record left behind in the rocks.

When tectonic plates collide they buckle at the edges as one plate is forced under the other. Where they buckle at the edges under the force of the collision they form mountain ranges, as great folds are formed which sink and rise again. The Alps were formed when Africa collided with Europe, while the Himalayas, which formed when India crashed into Asia 45 million years ago, are still rising as the two plates continue to push together – although only by about 5 mm each year. Depending on the type of rocks present in the Earth's crust in any one place, sometimes the crust does not fold – it simply shears to give a fault and a block mountain which is pushed up as a whole single block.

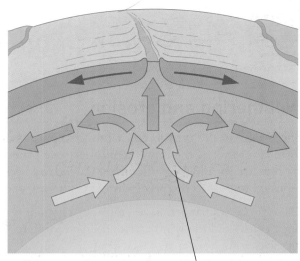

Hot magma rises and cools, pushing the plates apart.

↑ **Figure 2:** Radioactive decay deep within the Earth provides the energy which drives the tectonic plates over the Earth's surface.

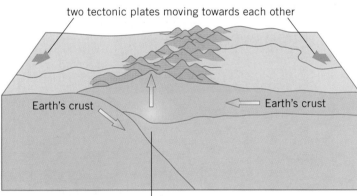

two tectonic plates moving towards each other

Earth's crust

Earth's crust

As the two plates push against each other, powerful forces produce high temperatures and enormous pressures. These melt the rock, and produce magma, which forces its way upwards, producing mountain ranges.

← **Figure 3:** The enormous temperatures and pressures which result from the formation of mountain ranges cause fundamental changes in the rocks making up the crust.

When mountain ranges are forming in this way, conditions of enormous heat and pressure build up within the rocks – up to 400 °C and 100 times atmospheric pressure. In these conditions the texture and mineral structure of both igneous rocks and sedimentary rocks may be changed *without* the rock ever becoming molten. Rocks which are changed in this way are known as metamorphic rocks, and the presence of such rocks is seen as evidence of mountain-building activity during the history of the Earth.

? Questions

1 The tectonic plates continue to move, even today. Sketch a diagram to show how you think the continents might be arranged on the surface of the Earth in 60 million years time. Label your sketch clearly to explain your ideas.

2 The presence of metamorphic rock is taken to show the presence of mountain-forming activity at some time in the history of the Earth. Why is this?

0── Key Ideas

⊙ Large scale movements of the Earth's crust cause mountain ranges to form very slowly over millions of years. These replace older mountain ranges worn down by weathering and erosion.

⊙ Metamorphic rocks are associated with Earth movements which created present-day and ancient mountain belts. They are formed as a result of the very high temperatures and pressures produced when tectonic plates push against each other.

Weathering and erosion

The surface of the Earth is constantly changing as new mountains and valleys form as a result of the movement of tectonic plates. At the same time as new features are forming, old mountain ranges and rocks are worn away and returned to dust in the processes of weathering and erosion.

These processes happen in several ways. The rain washes material away, ice forces open cracks and the wind carries soil and loose rock particles away. Acid rain dissolves some rock material, setting up chemical erosion. Sand particles carried in the wind, particularly in desert and coastal regions, wear away rocks. Water in the form of rivers and the sea wears away massive amounts of rock, forming valleys, and glaciers do even more damage. Trampling by people and animals also adds to the damage. The result of all this weathering and erosion is that rocks which we would otherwise be quite unaware of become exposed on the surface of the Earth. At the same time, much of the material removed by weathering is deposited as sediments to begin the process of formation of sedimentary rocks all over again (see the rock cycle in Section 5.4).

Figure 1: A zeugen (above) is a mushroom shaped rock which results from the blasting effect of sand blown along by the wind about a metre above the ground, or the action of sea water or melting glaciers. On Dartmoor (left), piles of granite are left exposed after wind and rain have worn away the hillside that once surrounded them. These are both clear examples of the effect weathering and erosion can have on rocks.

The moving crust

As the Earth's surface is eroded away, younger sedimentary rocks are usually found lying on top of older rocks. However sometimes sedimentary rock layers are found which are tilted, folded, fractured (faulted) and even turned upside down. When these layers are exposed as a result of weathering, they demonstrate very clearly that the Earth's crust is unstable and that it has been subjected to very large forces as it has moved and twisted. Often the movement of the sedimentary rock layers brings fossils to the surface – fossils which would otherwise remain hidden, buried deep within the crust of the Earth. By dating the rocks we can learn when the Earth movements occurred.

A marine organism dies and falls to the sea bed.

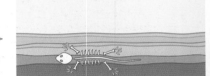

Layers of rock build up above the body of the organism – fossilisation occurs.

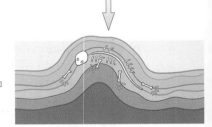

Rocks become folded.

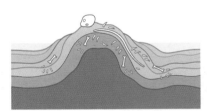

Erosion reveals the fossil.

A fault happens when two plates in the Earth's crust move in different directions. The relative movement may be vertical or horizontal, and sometimes it is even a combination of the two. When plates move relative to each other in this way the Earth's crust breaks, causing a **fracture**. The size of this fracture can range from virtually nothing up to several hundred kilometres (see Figure 4). Usually the movement

Figure 2: The tilted and folded layers of sedimentary rock not only tell us what has been happening to the Earth's crust – they can also reveal some of the secrets of early life on Earth, like this fossil shrimp which lived on Earth about 150 million years ago.

Finally, in 1869 the Russian scientist Dmitri Mendeleev cracked the problem. He arranged all of the 50 known elements of the time into a table. He placed them in the order of their atomic mass, and then arranged them so that a periodic pattern in their physical and chemical properties could be seen. His stroke of genius was to leave gaps for elements which were still to be discovered, predicting what their properties should be from his table. This was a tremendous publicity coup! A few years later, new elements were discovered with properties which matched almost exactly with Mendeleev's predictions – the case was won, and Dmitri Mendeleev went down in history as the man who first developed the periodic table.

⬇ **Figure 3:** It was the gaps which Mendeleev left in his periodic table – and the excitement which arose when they were filled – which meant that his peers took notice and recognised the value of his work.

From mass to number

Using the relative atomic mass of elements was the only option available to Mendeleev – the results it gave were good enough for the patterns to be recognised and accepted, but it had limitations. Although most of the elements are placed in the appropriate group using relative atomic mass, a few of them are not. For example, argon atoms have a greater atomic mass than potassium atoms. This meant that in Mendeleev's table, argon (an unreactive gas) was grouped with extremely reactive metals such as sodium and lithium, while potassium (an extremely reactive metal) was grouped with the unreactive gases. So argon fits better in front of potassium in the periodic table in terms of its properties. Discrepancies like this meant scientists felt that Mendeleev's table was not 100% reliable.

Once the structure of the atom was better understood, the modern periodic table was developed. We arrange the elements in order of their atomic (proton) number. This puts them all in exactly the right place and their patterns of physical and chemical properties reflect this. Now we have a reliable tool which provides us with an important summary of the structure of the atoms of all the elements.

Mendeleev's periodic table

Dmitri Mendeleev

? **Questions**

1 a What did Newlands base his classification on?

  b How was this different to the basis of Mendeleev's classification?

2 The development of an accurate periodic table has depended on the growth of chemical knowledge. Explain how the development of ideas in chemistry made the development of the modern periodic table possible.

3 Why has the periodic table been regarded as a reliable source of information since it has been based on the atomic number of elements?

4 As new elements have been discovered they have taken the places already waiting for them in the periodic table. How is this useful for scientists?

Patterns in the periodic table

Group 0

Groups

| 1 | 2 | | | | | | | | | | | | | 3 | 4 | 5 | 6 | 7 | |

mass number — 1 **H**
atomic (proton) number — 1

Groups

Groups 1	2													3	4	5	6	7	0
																			4 **He** 2
7 **Li** 3	9 **Be** 4													11 **B** 5	12 **C** 6	14 **N** 7	16 **O** 8	19 **F** 9	20 **Ne** 10
23 **Na** 11	24 **Mg** 12													27 **Al** 13	28 **Si** 14	31 **P** 15	32 **S** 16	35 **Cl** 17	40 **Ar** 18
39 **K** 19	40 **Ca** 20	45 **Sc** 21	48 **Ti** 22	51 **V** 23	52 **Cr** 24	55 **Mn** 25	56 **Fe** 26	59 **Co** 27	59 **Ni** 28	63 **Cu** 29	64 **Zn** 30	70 **Ga** 31	73 **Ge** 32	75 **As** 33	79 **Se** 34	80 **Br** 35	84 **Kr** 36		
85 **Rb** 37	88 **Sr** 38	89 **Y** 39	91 **Zr** 40	93 **Nb** 41	96 **Mo** 42	**Tc** 43	101 **Ru** 44	103 **Rh** 45	106 **Pd** 46	108 **Ag** 47	112 **Cd** 48	115 **In** 49	119 **Sn** 50	122 **Sb** 51	128 **Te** 52	127 **I** 53	131 **Xe** 54		
133 **Cs** 55	137 **Ba** 56	139 **La** 57	178 **Hf** 72	181 **Ta** 73	184 **W** 74	186 **Re** 75	190 **Os** 76	192 **Ir** 77	195 **Pt** 78	197 **Au** 79	201 **Hg** 80	204 **Tl** 81	207 **Pb** 82	209 **Bi** 83	**Po** 84	**At** 85	**Rn** 86		
Fr 87	226 **Ra** 88	227 **Ac** 89																	

Elements 58–71 and 90–103 (all metals) have been omitted.

Key

Reactive metals These metals react vigorously with other elements like oxygen or chlorine, and with water. They are all soft – some of them can even be cut with a knife, like cheese!

Transition metals This group contains the elements that most people probably think of when the word 'metal' is mentioned, like iron, copper, silver and gold. These metals are not usually very reactive – some, like silver and gold, are so unreactive that they are sometimes called 'noble metals'.

Less reactive metals This group is generally much less reactive than the reactive metals.

Non-metals These elements have low melting and boiling points, and many are liquids or gases at room temperature and pressure.

Noble gases These (non-metal) elements are very unreactive, and it is very difficult to get them to combine with other elements.

↑ **Figure 1:** The periodic table – each element is represented by its chemical symbol, with the relative atomic mass and proton number to one side. (Notice that most of the elements are metals – in all, fewer than one-quarter of the elements are non-metals.)

The periodic table is an arrangement of elements in terms of their electronic structure and their observed properties. There are two different patterns within the periodic table, and both of them are useful to us in different ways.

Filling up the shells

The horizontal rows of the periodic table are known as **periods**. As we move across a period of the table, each successive element has one more electron in its outer shell (or energy level) than the element before it. This carries on until the elements at the far right of the table all have completely full outer energy levels, so these elements are very stable and unreactive.

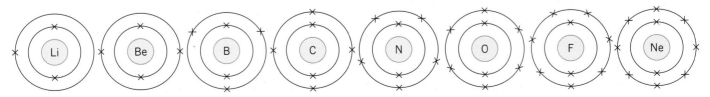

↑ **Figure 2:** As a period builds up, the number of electrons in the outer shell of each element increases by one. This example shows Period 2.

Moving down the groups

The vertical columns of the modern periodic table are called **groups** – Group 1, Group 2, etc. The elements in each group share similar properties. This is because they all have the same number of electrons in their outer energy levels.

The properties of elements are decided by how many electrons they have, and most importantly by the number of electrons in the outer energy level. The similarities and differences between elements in the same group of the periodic table can be explained by the electronic structure of their atoms. The elements in a group are similar because they have the same number of electrons in their outer energy level. They differ because each one has a different number of lower (inner) energy levels.

H Elements in the same group of the periodic table have similar properties because they have the same number of electrons in the highest occupied (outer) energy level. It is the number of lower energy levels underneath which then affect the detailed properties of the elements in one group. The higher the outer energy level is (that is, the more lower energy levels there are), the further the outer electrons are from the positive nucleus. This has two effects:

⊙ electrons are lost more easily because they are further from the pull of the positive nucleus

⊙ electrons are gained less easily because they are further from the attraction of the positive nucleus.

This explains many of the trends in reactivity which you will see in the following pages.

↓ **Figure 3:** All the elements in Group 1 react vigorously with water, but the reaction gets more violent moving down the group, as the number of inner energy levels changes.

lithium reacting with water

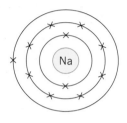

potassium reacting with water

? Questions

1 What is the difference between a period and a group of the periodic table?

2 Look at Figure 2.

  a What is the main difference in the electronic structure of lithium and fluorine?

  b Why is neon so unreactive?

H 3 Explain why the elements in Group 7 get *less* reactive as they go down the group, not more reactive.

🔑 Key Ideas

⊙ The periodic table shows the elements in order of atomic number – it is an arrangement based on the electronic structure of elements.

⊙ Horizontal rows are called periods, and moving across a period from left to right a particular energy level is gradually filled up.

⊙ Elements in a group all have the same number of electrons in their outer energy level.

⊙ Elements in a group have similar properties because they have the same numbers of electrons in the outer shell.

H ⊙ The higher the outer energy level the more easily electrons are lost and the less easily they are gained.

6.3 Group 1 – the alkali metals

The first group of the periodic table is known as the **alkali metals**. It includes the metals **lithium**, **sodium**, **potassium**, rubidium, caesium and francium. The first three are the only ones you will usually have to deal with, as the others are frighteningly reactive – and in the case of francium, radioactive as well!

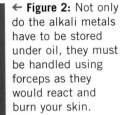

← **Figure 1:** The alkali metals make up Group 1 of the periodic table.

The properties of the alkali metals

All of the Group 1 metals are very reactive – they have to be stored in oil to stop them reacting with the oxygen in the air. The reactivity increases as we move down the group, so lithium is the least reactive alkali metal and francium the most reactive.

All of these metals have a very low density – lithium, sodium and potassium are less dense than water, so they all float on water. The alkali metals are also all very soft – they can be cut with a knife. They have the silvery, shiny look of typical metals when they are first cut, but they quickly go dull as they react with the air to form a white layer of oxide. The Group 1 metals also melt and boil at relatively low temperatures (for metals) and moving down the group the melting and boiling points get lower and lower.

All of the properties of this rather unusual group of metals are the result of their electronic structure. The alkali metals all have one electron in their outer energy level, which gives them similar properties. It also makes them very reactive, as they only need to lose one electron to obtain a stable outer energy level. They react with non-metals, losing their single electron and forming a metal ion carrying a +1 charge, eg Na^+, K^+. They always form ionic compounds.

← **Figure 2:** Not only do the alkali metals have to be stored under oil, they must be handled using forceps as they would react and burn your skin.

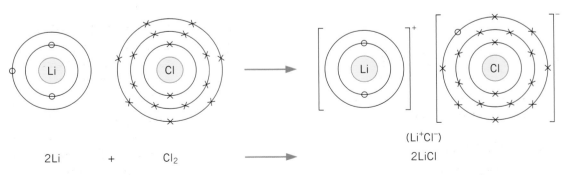

2Li   + Cl_2 ⟶   (Li^+Cl^-)
2LiCl

← **Figure 3:** The reaction between lithium and chlorine shows clearly the way that the alkali metals form positive ions when they react with non-metals.

Understanding the trends

While all of the alkali metals react in similar ways as a result of the single electron in their outer energy level, there are some definite trends in reactivity which can only be explained by looking in more detail at the structure of the atoms.

Density *increases* down the group as the atoms get bigger.

Melting points and boiling points *decrease* down the group because the metallic bonds between the electrons and the positive nuclei get less as the atoms get larger.

Reactivity *increases* – as the atoms get bigger, the outer electron is held less tightly by attraction to the positive nucleus because it is screened by other layers of electrons. This means the outer electron is lost more easily, so the element is more reactive.

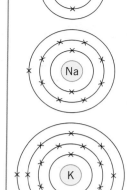

→ **Figure 4:** The trends in the properties we can observe moving down Group 1 of the periodic table are explained by the structure of the atoms themselves.

? Questions

1 Explain the following properties of Group 1 metals:

   a they have to be stored in oil

   b they need to be handled with forceps

   c they are shiny grey when they are first cut but soon go dull.

2 Why are the elements caesium, rubidium and francium not brought out in the laboratory and reacted with water?

3 Look at Figure 5.

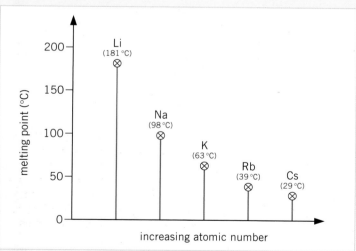

← **Figure 5:** The melting points of the Group 1 elements.

   a What is the melting point of lithium?

   b What is the melting point of rubidium?

   c What is the trend in melting points shown on the graph?

   d Sketch a graph to show the pattern you would expect in the boiling points of the Group 1 elements. The boiling point of lithium is 1342°C.

🔑 Key Ideas

⊙ The elements in Group 1 of the periodic table are known as the alkali metals.

⊙ The alkali metals are reactive, soft and have a low density.

⊙ The alkali metals form ions with a charge of +1 when they react with non-metals.

⊙ In Group 1, the further down the group an element is, the more reactive it is.

⊙ In Group 1, the further down the group, the lower the melting and boiling point of the element.

H ⊙ The higher the energy level of the outermost electrons, the more easily they are lost – this explains the increase in reactivity seen moving down the elements in Group 1.

6.4 Reactions of the alkali metals

Because the alkali metals all have a single electron in their outer energy level, they all react in a similar way with other elements and compounds. As they are so reactive, they are rarely used as metals. However, the compounds they make are very stable indeed and many of them are very useful.

The alkali metals react with different non-metals in very typical ways, allowing us to predict what might happen in a reaction we have never seen before. All we need to remember is that the more reactive the Group 1 metal, the more vigorous the reaction is likely to be!

Reactions with water

When a piece of lithium, sodium or potassium is added to water, the metal floats on the top, moving around and fizzing furiously. Heat is released in the reaction – sodium and potassium get so hot that they melt. The fizzing is caused because the metal reacts with the water to form hydrogen gas, which fizzes as it is given off, and a metal hydroxide. The hydroxides of the alkali metals are soluble, so they dissolve in the water and a colourless metal hydroxide solution results. These solutions are all alkalis – sodium hydroxide (NaOH) and potassium hydroxide (KOH) are examples. This is how the alkali metals get their name – they all form alkalis when they react with water!

$$2Na(s) + 2H_2O(l) \longrightarrow 2NaOH(aq) + H_2(g)$$
$$2K(s) + 2H_2O(l) \longrightarrow 2KOH(aq) + H_2(g)$$

The more reactive the metal, the more vigorously it reacts with water. The reaction with potassium, for example, gets hot enough to ignite the hydrogen which is formed.

Evidence for the reaction

Two observations show what is happening in the reaction between an alkali metal and water. All alkali metals react with water to produce hydrogen gas. When sodium and lithium react with water the hydrogen produced can be made to burn using a lighted splint. But the reaction between potassium and water is so vigorous that the heat produced by the reaction ignites the hydrogen without the need for a lighted splint.

The production of an alkaline solution can be shown by adding an indicator to the water (see Section 7.1). If universal indicator solution is used, it will turn green when added to the water before the reaction, showing that it is neutral. As the alkali metal reacts with the water the universal indicator will turn purple, showing the production of an alkaline solution due to hydroxide ions.

Reactions with oxygen

The alkali metals react with oxygen to form metal oxides. They burn in air with very attractive coloured flames. Each metal has a particular coloured flame. However, the oxides which are produced in these reactions are all white solids – not easy to tell apart just from their appearance.

$$4Li(s) + O_2(g) \longrightarrow 2Li_2O(s)$$
$$4K(s) + O_2(g) \longrightarrow 2K_2O(s)$$

↑ **Figure 1:** The reaction between alkali metals and water is a very vigorous one, and the more reactive the metal, the more vigorous the reaction!

Safety note: The test usually used to show that a colourless gas is hydrogen is to collect some in a test tube. When the gas is lit, hydrogen burns with an explosion that is described as a 'squeaky pop'. However, it is not safe to use a test tube to collect the hydrogen in this case, since the heat of the reaction may ignite the gas as it is being collected.

↓ **Figure 2:** Bright red for lithium, bright orange for sodium and bright lilac for potassium – these are the typical colours when these alkali metals are burned in air.

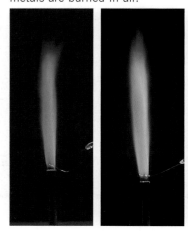

The oxides of the alkali metals all form alkaline solutions in water, just like the hydroxides. Both the oxides and the hydroxides react with acids to form compounds called *salts*. Examples of salts are lithium chloride (LiCl) and potassium chloride (KCl):

$$Li_2O + 2HCl \longrightarrow 2LiCl + H_2O$$
$$KOH + HCl \longrightarrow KCl + H_2O$$

Reactions with chlorine

The alkali metals also react vigorously with other non-metals such as chlorine. They produce metal chlorides – white solids which all dissolve readily in water to form colourless solutions.

The alkali metals react in a similar way with fluorine, bromine and iodine.

All of the compounds of the alkali metals are ionic, so they form crystals which dissolve easily in water.

↑ **Figure 3:** Two very reactive and dangerous substances – sodium and chlorine – react together vigorously to form a very stable ionic compound – sodium chloride, more commonly known as salt:

$$2Na + Cl_2 \longrightarrow 2NaCl$$

? Questions

1 Why are the Group 1 metals often known as the alkali metals?

2 An alkali metal is burned in air. The reaction produces a bright orangey yellow flame.

   a Which metal is being burnt in air?

   b Write a word equation for the reaction.

   c Write a balanced chemical equation for the reaction.

3 The reaction between sodium and chlorine is shown in Figure 3. How would you expect the reaction between the following pairs of elements to differ from this?

   a lithium and chlorine   b caesium and chlorine

4 Give balanced equations for the following reactions:

   a lithium + water   b caesium + water

   c the 'squeaky pop' reaction between hydrogen and the oxygen in the air.

5 Write balanced equations for the reaction between:

   a lithium and chlorine   b caesium and oxygen

   c rubidium and chlorine   d potassium and fluorine

   e sodium and bromine.

H 6 a Use data from Figure 4 to produce a table showing the radius of the ions of the elements in Group 1.

   b Explain the trend you observe in the ionic radius.

   c Explain the effect of this trend on the reactivity of the alkali metals.

0—π Key Ideas

⊙ The alkali metals react with water releasing hydrogen and forming soluble, alkaline metal hydroxides.

⊙ The alkali metals react readily with non-metals to form ionic compounds in which the metal ion carries a +1 charge.

⊙ The compounds are white solids which form colourless solutions in water.

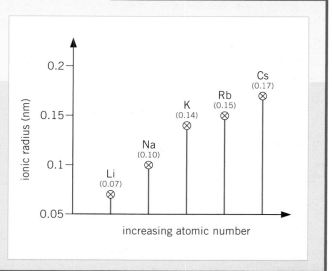

→ **Figure 4:** The ionic radius of the elements in Group 1.

6.5 Group 7 – the halogens

The **halogens** are a group of poisonous non-metals which all have coloured vapour. They are fairly typical non-metals with low melting and boiling points and they are poor conductors of heat and electricity. The best known members of the group are **fluorine**, **chlorine**, **bromine** and **iodine**.

Getting to know the halogens

The halogens are a varied group of elements in their physical appearance. At room temperature fluorine is a very reactive, poisonous yellow gas. Chlorine is a fairly reactive, poisonous dense green gas. It is important to be able to detect chlorine if it is given off. Chlorine has a distinctive smell, but there is a far safer test. Hold damp litmus paper in the unknown gas – if the litmus paper bleaches, the gas is chlorine.

Bromine is a dense, poisonous red-brown liquid which vaporises easily – it is volatile – while iodine is a poisonous dark grey crystalline solid. Iodine is used as an antiseptic because it is poisonous to bacteria, but it would poison us too if we swallowed it! The halogens take part in a wide range of reactions, many of which have to be carried out in a fume cupboard because the elements themselves are so poisonous.

As with all the groups of elements in the periodic table, there are patterns in the physical properties of the halogens.

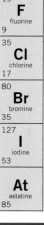

19	
F	fluorine
9	
35	
Cl	chlorine
17	
80	
Br	bromine
35	
127	
I	iodine
53	

← **Figure 1:** The halogens make up Group 7 of the periodic table.

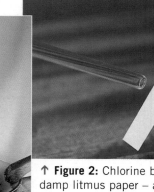

↑ **Figure 2:** Chlorine bleaches damp litmus paper – a reliable laboratory test for the presence of the gas.

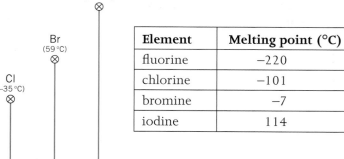

↑ **Figure 3:** Iodine appears to change straight from a solid to a gas when heated – the data in Figure 4 should help you to explain why.

Element	Melting point (°C)
fluorine	−220
chlorine	−101
bromine	−7
iodine	114

← **Figure 4:** The trends in the physical properties of the halogens can be seen clearly from data like these.

Moving down the group of the halogens, the melting and boiling points get higher – this explains the change from gas to liquid to solid at room temperature, from fluorine through chlorine and bromine to iodine.

Down to basics

The way the halogens react with other elements and compounds is a direct result of their electronic structure. They all have a relatively full outer energy level containing seven electrons, so they need one more electron to achieve a stable arrangement. Because of this arrangement they can and do take part in both ionic and covalent bonding.

↓ **Figure 5:** The halogens all exist as molecules made up of pairs of atoms.

 F_2

 Cl_2

 Br_2

 I_2

Ionic bonding in the halogens

The halogens all react with metals, gaining a single electron to give them a stable arrangement of electrons in the outer level, and forming ions with a −1 charge, eg F⁻, Cl⁻, I⁻. In these reactions salts known as metal halides are formed. Examples of the compounds formed are sodium chloride (NaCl), iron bromide ($FeBr_3$) and magnesium iodide (MgI_2).

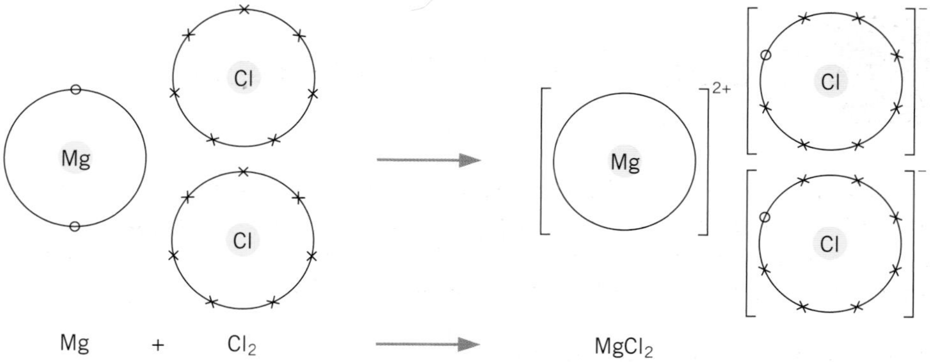

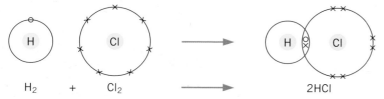

Mg   + Cl_2 $MgCl_2$

↑ **Figure 6:** When a halogen and a metal react, the metal donates electrons to the halogen and ionic bonds are formed between the resulting ions. (Only the outer energy levels are shown here.)

Covalent bonding in the halogens

When the halogens react with themselves or with other non-metals, they share electrons to gain a stable outer energy level and so they form covalent bonds (see Section 1.8). Examples of these compounds are the halogen molecules (F_2, Cl_2, etc), hydrogen chloride (HCl) and tetrachloromethane (CCl_4, also known as carbon tetrachloride).

H_2 + Cl_2 2HCl

↑ **Figure 7:** When a halogen and a non-metal react, they share electrons to form covalent bonds within the resulting molecules.

Hydrogen chloride is a dense colourless gas with a choking smell. Unlike many covalent compounds it dissolves readily in water to form hydrochloric acid. As it reacts with the water hydrogen ions and chloride ions are formed. It is these hydrogen ions which make the solution acidic.

$$HCl(g) \xrightarrow{\text{water}} H^+(aq) + Cl^-(aq)$$

Hydrogen fluoride, hydrogen bromide and hydrogen iodide all react in the same way with water – they are a family of very strong acids.

Key Ideas

- ⊙ The Group 7 elements are called the halogens.

- ⊙ The halogens have typical non-metal properties – they have low melting and boiling points and they are poor conductors of heat and electricity.

- ⊙ The halogens consist of molecules made up of pairs of atoms.

- ⊙ Halogens form ionic compounds when they react with metals (forming ions with a charge of −1) and covalent compounds when they react with non-metals.

? Questions

1 Produce a table to compare the properties of the halogens, from fluorine to iodine. Include in your table melting point, boiling point, state at room temperature and appearance.

2 Draw a graph to display the data given in the table (Figure 4).

3 Explain clearly the way in which the reactions of the halogens with metals differ from the reactions of the halogens with non-metals.

4 Produce dot and cross diagrams, along with balanced equations, for the following reactions between halogens and metals:

  a chlorine and magnesium

  b iodine and sodium

  c fluorine and aluminium

  d bromine and potassium.

5 Produce dot and cross diagrams, along with balanced equations, for the following reactions between halogens and non-metals:

  a fluorine atoms and hydrogen atoms

  b chlorine atoms and carbon atoms

  c chlorine atoms and iodine atoms

  d two bromine atoms.

Reactions of the halogens

It is not just the physical properties of the halogens which show a clear trend. The chemical reactivity of the elements changes too – they become less reactive moving down the group.

This change in reactivity becomes very clear when the reactions of the halogens with another element are observed. For example, when we look at the reactions of the halogens with hydrogen (Figure 1) very clear differences can be seen. The change from the explosive reaction of fluorine with hydrogen, to the slow and reversible reaction which takes place between iodine and hydrogen even at 300 °C and with a platinum catalyst, demonstrates clearly that the halogens become less reactive moving down the group.

Reaction of halogen with hydrogen	Conditions
Fluorine $F_2(g) + H_2(g) \rightarrow 2HF(g)$	explosive under all conditions
Chlorine $Cl_2(g) + H_2(g) \rightarrow 2HCl(g)$	explosive in sunlight — slow in dark
Bromine $Br_2(g) + H_2(g) \rightarrow 2HBr(g)$	300 °C + platinum catalyst
Iodine $I_2(g) + H_2(g) \rightleftharpoons 2HI(g)$	300 °C + platinum catalyst very slow and reversible

↑ **Figure 1:** The reactions of the halogens with hydrogen.

Displacement reactions

The more reactive halogens at the top of the group will displace the less reactive halogens from solutions of their salts. Bromine displaces iodine from solution because it is more reactive than iodine, whilst chlorine will displace both iodine and bromine. Obviously fluorine, the most reactive of the halogens, would displace all of the others, but because it reacts so strongly with water the displacement reactions cannot be carried out.

These displacement reactions take place between ions in solution. Although the halogens are easy to identify as elements because of their very different appearances, many of the metal halides form colourless solutions in water. To enable us to be sure which halide ion is present, there is a simple test involving silver nitrate. The nitrate ions displace the halide ions, forming silver halides. These are insoluble, so a silver halide precipitate is formed. For example:

silver nitrate + sodium chloride ⟶ silver chloride + sodium nitrate

$AgNO_3(aq) + NaCl(aq) \longrightarrow AgCl(s) + NaNO_3(aq)$

↑ **Figure 2:** Chlorine gas bubbled through potassium bromide solution displaces bromine from the solution:

$Cl_2 + 2KBr \longrightarrow 2KCl + Br_2$

The reddish brown colour of the bromine can be clearly seen in this photograph.

→ **Figure 3:** Silver chloride is white, silver bromide is cream and silver iodide is pale yellow. The colour of the precipitate allows us to identify the halide in the original solution.

Explaining the patterns

The patterns of behaviour of the elements in Group 7 can be explained by the arrangement of electrons in their highest occupied or outer energy level. The trend for the halogens is the opposite to that for the alkali metals. Moving down the group the elements become less reactive because electrons are gained, for ionic or covalent bonding, less and less easily. This is because the larger the atom becomes, the more layers of electrons there are screening the outer electrons from the attractive positive force of the nucleus. This means that the tendency to attract electrons gets less and less.

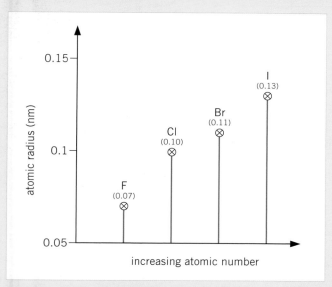

← **Figure 4:** The atomic radius of the halogen atoms gets larger moving down the group so electrons are gained less easily.

? Questions

1 Give a word equation and a balanced chemical equation for the reaction of:

  a fluorine   **b** iodine

  with hydrogen, showing the conditions under which the reactions take place.

2 **a** Explain why chlorine will displace bromine and iodine from solutions of their salts.

  b Give word and balanced chemical equations for the reactions between:

    i bromine and potassium iodide

    ii chlorine and magnesium bromide.

3 **a** Give balanced equations for the reactions between:

    i silver nitrate solution and potassium bromide

    ii silver nitrate solution and sodium iodide.

  b Explain how these reactions can be used to help identify an unknown solution.

4 Using the information given in Figure 4, explain the trend in the reactivity of the halogens down the group. Diagrams will make the explanation clearer.

Key Ideas

⊙ In Group 7, the further down the group an element is, the less reactive it will be and the higher its melting and boiling point will be.

⊙ A more reactive halogen can displace a less reactive halogen from an aqueous solution of its salt.

⊙ The decreased reactivity of halogens down the group is explained by the increased number of energy levels screening the outer electrons from the positive nucleus, so electrons are less easily gained down the group.

6.7 Group 0 – the noble gases

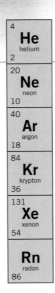

The elements in Group 0 of the periodic table are known as the **noble gases**. Another name for them is the *inert* gases, which is very appropriate as this group of elements is extremely inert (unreactive).

The non-reacting elements

Helium, neon, argon, along with krypton, xenon and radon are the least reactive elements known. It is very difficult to make them react with any other elements. They don't even react with themselves to form molecules. Most gases which are elements are diatomic – two atoms joined together to form a molecule. But the noble gases are monatomic – they exist as individual atoms because they will not form bonds of any sort with anything. So they are found simply as He, Ne, Ar, etc.

← **Figure 1**: The noble or inert gases make up Group 0 of the periodic table.

Why are the noble gases so unreactive?

As in so much of the chemistry of the periodic table, the reason for the unreactive character of the noble gases lies in their electronic structure. The outer electron energy level of a noble gas atom is full. The atoms are therefore completely stable – they have no tendency to gain, lose or share electrons.

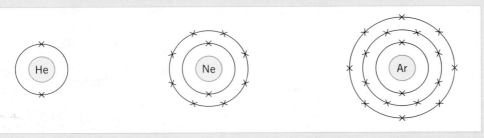

← **Figure 2**: The electronic structure of the noble gases explains their completely inert behaviour.

Typical non-metals

The noble gases are typical non-metals in many ways. They are colourless, odourless gases which have low melting and boiling points. They are poor conductors of heat and electricity, even when in the liquid form. Just like in other groups of the periodic table, there are clear trends in the melting and boiling points of the noble gases. The melting and boiling points increase down the group – although as the boiling point of radon is still only −62 °C, they all boil at pretty low temperatures.

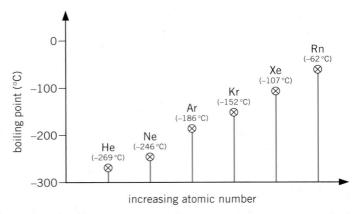

↑ **Figure 3**: The trend in the boiling point of the noble gases moving down the group can be clearly seen from this data.

The density of the noble gases also increases going down the group, the result of the atoms getting bigger all the time. Helium has the smallest and lightest atoms and so helium gas is less dense than air, a fact which is important when we look at its uses.

Gas	Density (g/dm³)
helium	0.17
neon	0.84
argon	1.66
krypton	3.49
xenon	5.47

← **Figure 4**: The density of the noble gases (at room temperature and pressure).

Using the noble gases

The noble gases do not take part in chemical reactions so we cannot use them to make useful materials for us. Instead, we use them in situations where their extreme lack of reactivity is useful in itself.

Helium is used in airships and in party balloons. Its low density means that it floats in air and its low reactivity means that it does not catch fire, unlike the only alternative gas, hydrogen. It is also used with oxygen as a breathing mixture for deep sea divers, as it reduces their chances of suffering from the 'bends'.

Neon is used in electrical discharge tubes – better known as neon lights. An electrical current is passed through the neon gas and it gives out a bright light as the electrons are excited without undergoing any chemical reaction. Neon lights are familiar as street lighting and in advertising. **Argon** is used in a different type of lighting – the everyday light bulb (or filament lamp). The argon provides an inert atmosphere so that when the electric current passes through the metal filament, making it very hot indeed, no chemical reaction takes place between the filament and the gas it is surrounded by. This stops the filament from burning away and makes light bulbs last longer. Helium, neon and argon are all used in lasers too.

↑ **Figure 5:** Helium balloons add colour and fun – yet are safe for the youngest child.

Key Ideas

- The elements of Group 0 are known as the noble gases.

- The noble gases are all chemically inert and exist as individual atoms.

- Their uses – in neon lights, filament lamps and balloons – all depend on their inert nature.

- The inert nature of the noble gases can be explained by their electronic structure.

Questions

1 a In what ways are the noble gases similar to the other non-metal elements?

  b In what ways do the noble gases differ from the other non-metal elements?

2 Draw a table to show the boiling points of the noble gases, using the data in Figure 3.

3 a Draw a graph of the data given in Figure 4.

  b What trend can you observe in the densities of the noble gases and how would you explain it?

4 How are the uses of the noble gases a reflection of their chemically inert nature?

The transition metals

In the centre of the periodic table there is a large block of metallic elements. They are known as the transition metals or transition elements. They include a wide variety of different elements, but many of them have characteristics in common.

45 **Sc** scandium 21	48 **Ti** titanium 22	51 **V** vanadium 23	52 **Cr** chromium 24	55 **Mn** manganese 25	56 **Fe** iron 26	59 **Co** cobalt 27	59 **Ni** nickel 28	63 **Cu** copper 29	64 **Zn** zinc 30
89 **Y** yttrium 39	91 **Zr** zirconium 40	93 **Nb** niobium 41	96 **Mo** molybdenum 42	55 **Tc** technetium 43	101 **Ru** ruthenium 44	103 **Rh** rhodium 45	106 **Pd** palladium 46	108 **Ag** silver 47	112 **Cd** cadmium 48
139 **La** lanthanum 57	178 **Hf** hafnium 72	181 **Ta** tantalum 73	184 **W** tungsten 74	186 **Re** rhenium 75	190 **Os** osmium 76	192 **Ir** iridium 77	195 **Pt** platinum 78	197 **Au** gold 79	201 **Hg** mercury 80
227 **Ac** actinium 89									

← **Figure 1:** The transition metals – the more common ones are shown in bold type.

Looking at the transition metals we do not find trends in the way that we did when we looked at the different groups of elements. However, they do have a number of important characteristics in common.

The properties of the transition metals

The transition metals have a typical metallic structure which explains most of their properties. The metals atoms exist in a giant structure held together by metallic bonds, and the outer electrons of each atom can move about freely within the metal.

Like all metals, the transition metals are very good conductors of electricity and heat – the free electrons carry the electrical current or the heat energy through the metal. The transition metals are also hard, tough and strong, yet they can easily be bent or hammered into useful shapes.

With the exception of mercury, which is a liquid at room temperature, the transition metals have very high melting points. This is very clear if they are compared to the alkali metals of Group 1.

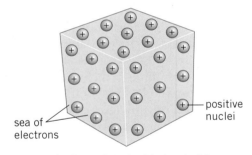

sea of electrons — positive nuclei

↑ **Figure 2:** It is this 'sea' of free electrons which explains many of the properties of typical metals.

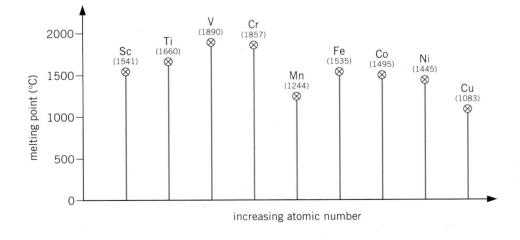

← **Figure 3:** Not only are the melting points of the transition elements generally much higher than those of the Group 1 elements (see Figure 5 on page 91), they also show much less variation.

The transition metals are much less reactive than the metals in Group 1. This means they do not react as easily with oxygen or water as the alkali metals – in other words, they only corrode very slowly. This makes the transition metals very useful as structural materials, particularly when they are mixed together or combined with other elements to make alloys. Iron mixed with carbon is certainly the best known of these (see Section 4.3). Other very useful combinations of transition metals are bronze, which is a combination of copper and tin, and cupro-nickel, the very hard alloy of copper and nickel which is used to make the coins we use in our currency.

Iron is the transition metal which is used most widely in the construction of buildings and vehicles. Copper, on the other hand, has another very important use. Copper is an excellent conductor of heat and electricity, and it can also be drawn out into long wires. Because of this it is very widely used for making electrical cables, and also for high quality cookware – it is a lot more expensive than the iron and steel usually used for cooking utensils. Copper is also used to make household water pipes, often replacing lead. Lead was used extensively for water pipes in the last century until people discovered it was poisonous – now old piping is being replaced with copper or plastic tubes to do the same job safely.

↑ **Figure 4:** Some of the transition metals which play so many important roles in our lives – copper (centre) and (clockwise from left) aluminium pellets, nickel–chrome ore, nickel bars, titanium rods, iron–nickel ore, niobium bars, chromium granules.

The transition metals have many properties in common, so what you know about one or two of the elements can be applied to almost any of them. Transition metals have some quite unusual properties which in turn influence the way we use them.

Coloured compounds

Many of the transition metals form coloured compounds. These include some very common compounds which we use in the laboratory. For example, potassium manganate (VII) is purple – the purple colour is due to the manganese ion in the compound. Similarly, copper (II) sulphate is blue (from the copper ion) and potassium chromate (VI) is orange (from the chromium ion). These colours are shown in Figure 1.

The colours which are produced by the transition elements are important in the world around us – for example, the colours of many minerals, rocks and gem stones are the result of transition metal ions. A reddish brown colour in the rocks is often the result of the iron ions, whilst the blue colour of sapphires and the green of emeralds are due to transition metal ions within the structure of the crystal.

People make use of the coloured ions of the transition metals in a variety of ways. Many of the glazes which are applied to pottery contain transition metal ions which are the basis of the colour they produce. Also as copper weathers it produces a green film of basic copper carbonate. This green patina is very attractive and is generally known as verdigris, and this is one reason why copper is used for many statues. The green colour is a direct result of the copper ions in the compound.

↓ **Figure 1:** The bright colours of these compounds are the result of the transition metal ions they contain.

↖ **Figure 2:** The colours which result from transition metal ions may be dull (like the verdigris on this statue), shiny or sparkly (like these sapphires), but they are almost always regarded as attractive and desirable.

H When compounds containing transition elements are written down they usually include a Roman number as well as the name of the compound, eg potassium manganate(VII), copper(II) sulphate. This is because transition metals often have more than one form of ion. Examples include iron (Fe^{2+} and Fe^{3+}), copper (Cu^+ and Cu^{2+}) and chromium (Cr^{2+} and Cr^{3+}). Some of the metals have even more – vanadium has five different types of ion! The interesting thing is that the different ions usually cause different colours in the compounds. For example, iron(II) ions (Fe^{2+}) give compounds with a green colour, whilst iron(III) ions (Fe^{3+}) are usually the reddish brown colour we associate with rust!

Convenient catalysts

Most chemical reactions take place quite slowly – in fact left alone most of the chemical reactions in the chemical industries would take place so slowly that we would never get enough of the chemicals we need, and the people running the companies would never make any money. Fortunately most reactions can be speeded up. This might be brought about by an increase in temperature or pressure, or it might depend on a **catalyst** (see Section 8.3).

Catalysts speed up a chemical reaction without being changed themselves in any way. They do not change the proportion of the products made, and they can often be reused time after time. Many of the transition elements make very effective catalysts. In the Haber process for making ammonia (see Sections 4.8 and 9.6) iron is used as a catalyst. Platinum and nickel are important catalysts in the process by which vegetable oils such as olive oil and corn oil are turned into margarine. Manganese(IV) oxide is the catalyst often used in the decomposition of hydrogen peroxide. Another increasingly important role for transition elements such as platinum is in the catalytic converters attached to car engines. These catalytic converters remove most of the pollutant gases, produced by the engine of a car as it burns petrol, before they reach the atmosphere, so transition elements in their role as catalysts are helping us to combat pollution.

← **Figure 3:** Transition metals, as catalysts within the catalytic converters fitted to all new cars, can help to make air pollution like this a thing of the past.

? Questions

1 a Give three examples of coloured transition metal compounds.

  b Give two examples of the role of coloured transition metal compounds in the natural world.

  c Give two examples of the ways in which people make use of coloured transition metal compounds.

2 a What is a catalyst?

  b Give examples of three transition metals which are used as catalysts and describe what they are used for.

⊙—m Key Ideas

- ⊙ Most transition metals form coloured compounds.

- ⊙ The coloured compounds can be seen in different coloured pottery glazes, in weathered copper and in gem stones.

- ⊙ Many transition metals, including iron and platinum, are used as catalysts.

1 The first airships were filled with hydrogen gas. Now helium gas is used in airships.

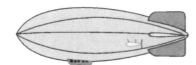

a The list gives some chemical symbols.

Ar   Cl   H   He   O

Choose from the list the correct chemical symbol for:

i hydrogen (1 mark)

ii helium. (1 mark)

b Choose **one** property from the list below which makes both hydrogen and helium useful for airships.

colourless   low density   no smell (1 mark)

c Explain why helium is now used in airships and why hydrogen is no longer used. (2 marks)

(Total 5 marks)

AQA specimen question

2 Part of the periodic table which Mendeleev published in 1869 is shown below.

	Group 1	Group 2	Group 3	Group 4	Group 5	Group 6	Group 7
Period 1	H						
Period 2	Li	Be	B	C	N	O	F
Period 3	Na	Mg	Al	Si	P	S	Cl
Period 4	K Cu	Ca Zn	* *	Ti *	V As	Cr Se	Mn Br
Period 5	Rb Ag	Sr Cd	Y In	Zr Sn	Nb Sb	Mo Te	* I

Use the periodic table at the back of the book to help you answer this question.

a Some elements in Group 1 of Mendeleev's periodic table are **not** found in Group 1 of the modern periodic table. Name **two** of these elements. (1 mark)

b Which group of elements in the modern periodic table is missing on Mendeleev's table? (1 mark)

c Mendeleev left several gaps in his periodic table. These gaps are shown as asterisks (*) on the table above. Suggest why Mendeleev left these gaps. (1 mark)

d Copy and complete the following sentence:

In the **modern** periodic table the elements are arranged in the order of their .... numbers. (1 mark)

(Total 4 marks)

AQA specimen question

3 One definition of an element is:

'A substance which cannot be broken down into simpler substances by chemical methods'.

The table shows some of the 'substances' which Antoine Lavoisier thought were elements. He divided the 'substances' into four groups. He published these groups in 1789.

The modern names of some of the substances are given in brackets.

Acid-making elements	Gas-like elements	Metallic elements	Earthy elements
sulphur	light	cobalt	lime (calcium oxide)
phosphorus	caloric (heat)	copper	magnesia (magnesium oxide)
charcoal (carbon)	oxygen	gold	barytes (barium sulphate)
	azote (nitrogen)	iron	argilla (aluminium oxide)
	hydrogen	lead	silex (silicon dioxide)
		manganese	
		mercury	
		nickel	
		platina (platinum)	
		silver	
		tin	
		tungsten	
		zinc	

a Name **one** 'substance' in the list which is **not** a chemical element or compound. (1 mark)

b **i** Name **one** 'substance' in the list which is a compound. (1 mark)

ii Suggest why Lavoisier thought that this 'substance' was an element. (1 mark)

c Dmitri Mendeleev devised a periodic table of the elements in 1869. A modern version of this table is shown at the back of the book.

Give **two** ways in which Mendeleev's table is more useful than Lavoisier's. (2 marks)

(Total 5 marks)

AQA specimen question

H 4 a The table gives the atomic numbers and boiling points of the noble gases.

Noble gas	Atomic number	Boiling point (°C)
helium	2	−269
neon	10	−246
argon	18	−186
krypton	36	
xenon	54	−107
radon	86	−62

i Draw a graph of boiling point against atomic number. Draw a line of best fit through the points. (3 marks)

ii Use the graph to help you complete the sentence.

The estimated boiling point of krypton is ...°C. (1 mark)

b Krypton is very unreactive.

i Explain, as fully as you can, why krypton is so unreactive. (3 marks)

ii Very few compounds of krypton have ever been made. One compound is krypton fluoride.

A sample of krypton fluoride was found to contain 0.42 g of krypton and 0.19 g of fluoride. Calculate the formula of krypton fluoride.

To gain full marks you must show all your working.

(Relative atomic masses: F = 19, Kr = 84) (4 marks)

(Total 11 marks)

AQA specimen question

H 5 a The transition elements have the typical properties of metals.

i Transition metals are good conductors of electricity.

Explain why. (2 marks)

ii Transition metals have high melting points.

Explain why. (2 marks)

b Iron is a transition metal. Iron, because of its strength, is used in the building of ship's hulls. The main problem with using iron is that it rusts unless protected.

Explain how attaching zinc blocks to an iron hull stops it from rusting. (2 marks)

(Total 6 marks)

AQA specimen question

H 6 Fluorine is more reactive than chlorine. Fluorine reacts with most elements in the periodic table. However, fluorine does not react with argon.

(Atomic numbers: F = 9, Cl = 17)

a To which group of the periodic table do fluorine and chlorine belong? (1 mark)

b Copy the diagram below. On your diagram, draw the electron arrangement of a chlorine atom. (2 marks)

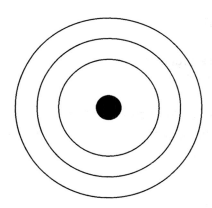

c Explain why fluorine is more reactive than chlorine. (3 marks)

(Total 6 marks)

AQA specimen question

Acids and bases

When a substance dissolves in water it forms an aqueous solution. That solution may be acidic, alkaline or neutral. **Bases** are chemicals which can neutralise **acids**, and **alkalis** are bases which dissolve in water. Pure water is neutral. To find out whether a given solution is acidic, basic or neutral we use a special chemical called an **indicator**.

Why are indicators important?

We need to be able to tell whether a solution is acidic, alkaline or neutral for a number of reasons. One is that during many chemical reactions, changes in acidity or alkalinity take place. If we can observe this change, then we can tell whether a reaction has happened at all, and whether it has finished or not. The other major reason why it is important for us to tell whether a solution is acidic or alkaline is safety. Both acids and alkalis are potentially dangerous chemicals which can break down and destroy not only clothing but human body tissues as well.

Acids

Acids include chemicals like citric acid, sulphuric acid and ethanoic acid. They all have a very sour taste, although many of them are too dangerous to put in your mouth. They are often used in chemical reactions in the laboratory, yet ethanoic acid (vinegar) and citric acid (the sour taste in citrus fruits, fizzy drinks and squashes) are examples of acids which we regularly eat.

One of the most commonly used laboratory acids is hydrochloric acid (HCl). This is formed when the gas hydrogen chloride dissolves in water. The other hydrogen halides – hydrogen fluoride, hydrogen bromide and hydrogen iodide – behave in a similar way, producing hydrofluoric, hydrobromic and hydroiodic acids respectively (Section 6.5).

$$HCl(g) \xrightarrow{\text{water}} H^+(aq) + Cl^-(aq)$$

Bases

Bases are the opposite of acids in the way they react. Because alkalis are bases which dissolve in water, they are the bases which are most commonly used. For example, ammonium hydroxide (NH_4OH), sodium hydroxide (NaOH) and potassium hydroxide (KOH) are often found in school laboratories. Ammonium hydroxide is formed when ammonia gas dissolves in water, the other two when solid sodium hydroxide or potassium hydroxide dissolve in water. They all form alkaline solutions. For example:

ammonia + water $\longrightarrow$ ammonium hydroxide
$$NH_3(g) + H_2O(l) \longrightarrow NH_4OH(aq)$$

sodium hydroxide + water $\longrightarrow$ sodium hydroxide
$$NaOH(s) + H_2O(l) \longrightarrow NaOH(aq)$$

↑ **Figure 1:** Acids can be dangerously corrosive. This is the apparatus worn by John Haigh, the Acid Bath Murderer, to protect himself from the sulphuric acid he used to dissolve the bodies of his victims.

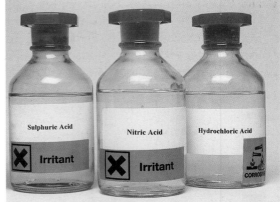

Sulphuric Acid — **Irritant** Nitric Acid — **Irritant** Hydrochloric Acid — **CORROSIVE**

↑ **Figure 2:** The three most common laboratory acids.

The ionic basis of acidic and alkaline solutions is quite simple:

- Acids are substances which form hydrogen ions (H^+) when added to water. Hydrogen ions make solutions acidic. For example:

$$H_2SO_4(aq) \longrightarrow 2H^+(aq) + SO_4^{2-}(aq)$$
$$HNO_3(aq) \longrightarrow H^+(aq) + NO_3^-(aq)$$

- Alkalis are substances which form hydroxide ions (OH^-) when added to water. Hydroxide ions make solutions alkaline. For example:

$$NH_4OH(aq) \longrightarrow NH_4^+(aq) + OH^-(aq)$$
$$NaOH(aq) \longrightarrow Na^+(aq) + OH^-(aq)$$

Like strong acids, strong alkalis are corrosive and cause great damage to the skin by reacting with the fats and oils found in it. Both acids and alkalis only show their properties when they are dissolved in water.

Using indicators

Many acids and alkalis look very similar – most of them form colourless solutions so telling them apart would be very difficult without indicators. Indicators are special chemicals which change colour with acids and alkalis. Litmus paper is a well known indicator but there are many more, including some natural ones like the juice of red cabbage or beetroot.

The pH scale

We use the pH scale to tell us the strength of an acid or alkali. It runs from 1 (the strongest acid) to 14 (the strongest alkali). Universal indicator is a very special indicator made up of a number of dyes. It turns different colours in different strengths of acid and alkali. Anything in the middle of the pH scale (pH 7) is neutral – neither acid nor alkali.

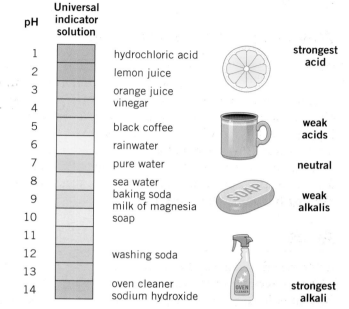

↑ **Figure 3:** The pH scale.

Universal indicator is also used in pH papers, which give different colours.

 Questions

1 Why is it important to be able to find out if a colourless solution is acidic, basic or neutral?

2 a What is an indicator?

 b What is the pH scale?

 c How are indicators and the pH scale linked?

3 When the gas hydrogen fluoride reacts with water, a very unpleasant acid is formed. Give a word and balanced chemical equation for the formation of hydrofluoric acid.

4 When potassium hydroxide dissolves in water an alkaline solution is formed. Give a word and balanced chemical equation for this reaction.

Key Ideas

- When a substance dissolves in water it forms an aqueous solution which may be acidic, alkaline or neutral.

- Pure water is neutral.

- Hydrogen halides are gases which dissolve in water to produce acidic solutions.

- Ammonia dissolves in water to form an alkaline solution.

- H^+ ions make a solution acidic while OH^- ions make a solution alkaline.

- Indicators can be used to show if a solution is acidic, alkaline or neutral by the way the colours change.

- The pH scale is used to show how acidic or alkaline a solution is.

7.2 Neutralisation

When an acid reacts with a base or an alkali, it forms a neutral solution containing a salt and water. This is known as a **neutralisation** reaction. The general formula which describes all reactions of this type is:

acid + base $\longrightarrow$ salt + water

An indicator can be used to show when acidic and alkaline solutions have completely reacted to produce a neutral salt solution.

Examples of neutralisation reactions are:

hydrochloric acid + sodium hydroxide $\longrightarrow$ sodium chloride + water

$HCl(aq)$ + $NaOH(aq)$ $\longrightarrow$ $NaCl(aq)$ + $H_2O(l)$

sulphuric acid + ammonium hydroxide $\longrightarrow$ ammonium sulphate + water

$H_2SO_4(aq)$ + $NH_4OH(aq)$ $\longrightarrow$ $NH_4SO_4(aq)$ + $H_2O(l)$

↑ **Figure 1:** Universal indicator clearly shows that the acid and alkali have completely reacted together to form a neutral salt solution.

H Neutralisation reactions can be expressed in terms of what is happening to the acidic and alkaline ions. Hydrogen ions (H^+) combine with hydroxide ions (OH^-) to form water molecules:

$H^+(aq)$ + $OH^-(aq)$ $\longrightarrow$ $H_2O(l)$

Ideas and Evidence

Everyday acids and alkalis

Although we learn about acids and alkalis in the context of the science laboratory, they play an important role in everyday life. Some of their everyday uses are outlined below.

⊙ Both acids and alkalis are used as household and industrial cleaners.

Acids dissolve lime scale. The acid reacts with the calcium carbonates and magnesium carbonates in the lime scale to produce soluble salts, carbon dioxide and water. All of the lime scale removers for toilets, sinks, kettles, washing machines, dishwashers and irons are basically acids.

Alkalis react with and remove grease and fat. So soaps, detergents and oven cleaners are all alkalis.

⊙ The reaction between alkalis and fat is used to make soap. Traditionally sodium hydroxide was boiled up with animal fats, but now a wide range of fats and oils are used.

↑ **Figure 2:** The reaction of acids with lime scale gives us a vital tool in the battle against the build-up of scale in pipes, kettles, toilets and washing machines.

- Our stomach makes quite powerful hydrochloric acid to help break down our food. But too much of this acid causes indigestion. Indigestion tablets rely on the reaction between alkalis (such as magnesium oxide) and acid, neutralising the excess acid and ending the discomfort.

- The soil can become very acidic because of the action of microorganisms or as a result of acid rain. Spreading lime (calcium hydroxide) adds an alkali to the acid and neutralises the excess acid in the ground.

- Lakes can become very acidic because of acid rain. Again, adding the lime neutralises the excess acid and keeps the water safe for animals and plants to live in.

Science people

The big problem with measuring the acidity or alkalinity of a solution is that the concentration of hydrogen ions varies so much, from about $12 \, mol/dm^3$ at the high end to around $10^{-15} \, mol/dm^3$ at the low end. The problem caused by this awkward measuring system was solved in 1909 by a Danish chemist called Soren Peter Lauritz Sorensen, when he was working on methods to improve quality in the brewing industry. He suggested using a logarithmic scale for hydrogen ion concentration, which meant that the acidity or alkalinity could be measured using a simple scale running from 1 to 14. This is why the name pH is used – it stands for **p**ower of **H**ydrogen. Not surprisingly, Sorensen's idea was quickly welcomed and used by other chemists.

← **Figure 3:** Soren Sorensen, who made life easier for chemists everywhere!

Questions

1 When some fertilisers are added to soil they dissolve in the water in the soil and make it acidic. This means that some crops will not grow well in the soil. Farmers sometimes spread lime (calcium oxide, a base) over the soil after adding fertiliser to it.

   a Why do farmers spread lime on the soil?

   b What might happen if a farmer spreads too much lime onto the soil?

2 Write down the formulae of the following compounds:

   a lithium hydroxide   **d** potassium hydroxide

   b hydrochloric acid   **e** ammonium hydroxide

   c sulphuric acid   **f** nitric acid.

3 Give word and balanced chemical equations for the following neutralisation reactions:

   a hydrochloric acid and potassium hydroxide

   b nitric acid and sodium hydroxide

   c sulphuric acid and potassium hydroxide

   d hydrochloric acid and ammonium hydroxide.

H 4 For each of the reactions in question 3 show the neutralisation in terms of the *ions* involved. For example, for part **a**:

$$H^+ + Cl^- + K^+ + OH^- \longrightarrow KCl + H_2O$$

Key Ideas

- When an acid reacts with a base a neutralisation reaction takes place.

- An indicator can be used to show when acidic and alkaline solutions have completely reacted to produce a neutral salt solution.

H - In neutralisation reactions the H^+ of the acid reacts with the OH^- of the alkali to form neutral water (H_2O).

7.3 Making salts

The alkali metals from Group 1 of the periodic table have oxides and hydroxides which dissolve in water to make alkaline solutions – which is why they are known as the alkali metals. The metals in Group 2 of the periodic table – metals like calcium and magnesium – also have hydroxides and oxides which dissolve in water to produce alkalis, although they are not so strongly alkaline as those involving Group 1 metals.

When an alkaline solution reacts with an acid solution, the neutralisation reaction that occurs produces a salt and water:

acid + alkaline hydroxide solution ⟶ a neutral salt solution + water

Choosing a salt

By carefully choosing both the alkali and the acid, we can determine which salt will be made. The salt which results from a reaction depends on two things:

⊙ The metal in the alkali will determine which metal salt is produced. For example, if sodium hydroxide is used as the alkali, then whatever acid the alkali is reacted with, the salts produced will always be sodium salts.

⊙ The other factor is the acid used. When an alkali is reacted with **hydrochloric** acid to neutralise it, the salt formed will always be a **chloride**. Whatever alkali is reacted with **sulphuric** acid, the salt will always be a **sulphate**. Neutralising **nitric** acid always gives a **nitrate**.

In other words, it is the combination of the metal in the alkali and the acid used which decides which salt will be formed. For example:

hydro**chloric** acid + **potassium** hydroxide ⟶ **potassium chloride** + water

$HCl(aq)$ + $KOH(aq)$ ⟶ $KCl(aq)$ + $H_2O(l)$

sulphuric acid + **sodium** hydroxide ⟶ **sodium sulphate** + water

$H_2SO_4(aq)$ + $2NaOH(aq)$ ⟶ $Na_2SO_4(aq)$ + $2H_2O(l)$

nitric acid + **lithium** hydroxide ⟶ **lithium nitrate** + water

$HNO_3(aq)$ + $LiOH(aq)$ ⟶ $LiNO_3(aq)$ + $H_2O(l)$

The oxides of the transition metals are also bases, so very similar reactions take place when acids react with oxides. Again, a salt and water are the products of the reaction. For example:

sulphuric acid + zinc oxide ⟶ zinc sulphate + water

$H_2SO_4(aq)$ + $ZnO(aq)$ ⟶ $ZnSO_4(aq)$ + $H_2O(l)$

Making ammonium salts

Ammonium salts can be made in two ways. Ammonia may be bubbled through an acid – it forms an aqueous solution which combines with the acid to form an ammonium salt. For example:

hydrochloric acid + ammonia ⟶ ammonium chloride

$HCl(aq)$ + $NH_3(aq)$ ⟶ $NH_4Cl(aq)$

sulphuric acid + ammonia ⟶ ammonium sulphate

$H_2SO_4(aq)$ + $2NH_3(aq)$ ⟶ $(NH_4)_2SO_4(aq)$

↑ **Figure 1:** A soluble salt made by the reaction of an alkaline hydroxide solution with an acid can be extracted from the solution by evaporation of the water. This dish contains sodium chloride crystals.

copper sulphate crystal

zinc sulphate crystals

↑ **Figure 2:** If copper oxide and zinc are both reacted with sulphuric acid, the sulphates which result are easily distinguished!

On the other hand, the ammonia may be bubbled through water first to make ammonium hydroxide (see Section 7.1). This in turn reacts with an acid to give an ammonium salt and water. For example, with nitric acid:

ammonium hydroxide + nitric acid $\longrightarrow$ ammonium nitrate + water

$$NH_4OH(aq) + HNO_3(aq) \longrightarrow NH_4NO_3(aq) + H_2O(l)$$

The direct reaction of ammonia with nitric acid also gives ammonium nitrate, and these reactions are very important in the manufacture of nitrate fertilisers.

Ideas and Evidence

A special sort of salt!

When alkalis react with fatty acids, a very special type of neutralisation reaction takes place, and the 'sa.t' which is produced is what we know as soap! This reaction takes place when an alkali such as sodium hydroxide is boiled up with animal fats or vegetable oils, made up of long chain fatty acids:

alkali + fatty acid $\longrightarrow$ soap + water

Commercially the reaction is carried out in great 'soap kettles'. Brine is pumped into them after the fats and alkali have boiled, and the insoluble soap precipitates out as a curd on the top. The pure soap is taken and processed – perfumes and colours may be added – before it is packaged for sale.

The reaction between alkalis and fatty acids is not confined to the soap factory. The reason that alkalis are so dangerous is that if they are spilled on your skin they react with the fatty acids present in all of your cells, destroying the structure and forming 'human soap' which makes your skin feel slimy as the tissue is broken down!

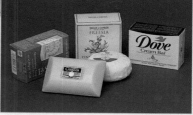

↑ **Figure 3:** Few people realise that the soaps they buy started life as a reacting mass of hot alkali mixed with animal fats or plant oils!

Questions

1 Give word and balanced chemical equations for the reactions between an acid and the hydroxide of an alkali metal which would result in the following salts:

  a lithium chloride

  b sodium nitrate

  c potassium sulphate.

2 State what salts you would expect from the following neutralisation reactions:

  a nitric acid and calcium hydroxide

  b nitric acid and ammonia

  c sulphuric acid and lithium hydroxide.

3 Explain why the making of soap can be described as a neutralisation reaction.

4 Design a leaflet, or produce a display to be put up in the laboratory, for the new intake of pupils in September giving them information about acids and alkalis and explaining why these should be treated with respect.

Key Ideas

⊙ The salts of alkali metals can be made by reacting solutions of their alkaline hydroxides with acids to form neutral salts and water.

⊙ The salt produced depends on the metal in the alkali and the acid used.

⊙ Neutralising hydrochloric acid produces chlorides.

⊙ Neutralising nitric acid produces nitrates.

⊙ Neutralising sulphuric acid produces sulphates.

Neutralisation reactions are not always as simple as adding a solution of a metal hydroxide to a solution of an acid. To make the salts of the transition metals we have to overcome the fact that although their oxides and hydroxides react with acids, they do not dissolve in water.

Making transition metal salts

The oxides and hydroxides of the transition metals are bases, so they will react with acids to form a salt and water. However, they will not dissolve in water, although the salts that are formed are usually soluble. To produce a soluble transition metal salt, the solid metal hydroxide (or oxide) is added to an acid until no more will react, so that the acid is completely neutralised. The excess metal hydroxide (or oxide) is then removed from the soluble salt solution by filtering, after which the soluble salt can be obtained by evaporation of the water. For example:

↓ **Figure 1:** This method of making salts is common for most of the transition elements because of their insoluble oxides and hydroxides.

$$\text{copper(II) oxide} + \text{sulphuric acid} \longrightarrow \text{copper(II) sulphate} + \text{water}$$
$$CuO(s) + H_2SO_4(aq) \longrightarrow CuSO_4(aq) + H_2O(l)$$

(a) Insoluble black copper oxide is added to a solution of sulphuric acid.

(b) As the reaction takes place the colourless acid solution turns blue, indicating the presence of copper sulphate.

(c) When the reaction is complete and all the acid is used up, the excess black copper oxide powder remains at the bottom.

(d) The solution of copper sulphate is filtered to remove the excess copper oxide.

(e) After evaporation of the water blue copper sulphate crystals are left.

Other transition metal salts are made in the same way, with the excess metal oxide or hydroxide always removed by filtering. The salt which is produced is determined by the metal in the hydroxide or oxide used and the acid which takes part in the reaction, just as for the other salts we have looked at (Section 7.3). For example:

$$\text{iron(III) oxide} + \text{hydrochloric acid} \longrightarrow \text{iron(III) chloride} + \text{water}$$
$$Fe_2O_3(s) + 6HCl(aq) \longrightarrow 2FeCl_3(aq) + 3H_2O(l)$$

$$\text{copper hydroxide} + \text{nitric acid} \longrightarrow \text{copper nitrate} + \text{water}$$
$$Cu(OH)_2(s) + 2HNO_3(aq) \longrightarrow Cu(NO_3)_2(aq) + 2H_2O(l)$$

The silver halides

The silver halides are a group of silver salts, silver being one of the most unreactive transition metals. The silver halides (silver chloride, silver bromide and silver iodide) are all relatively unstable, so the compounds are very easily split up (decomposed). In fact, the energy from ordinary visible light is sufficient to cause the silver halides to decompose to give silver and the halogen (chlorine, bromine or iodine). Because of this silver halides are used to make photographic film and photographic paper. Silver bromide and silver iodide are most commonly used.

When a photographic film is exposed to light, a reaction known as **photochemical decomposition** takes place. The silver ions in the silver halide are reduced to silver atoms, whilst the halide ions are oxidised to form halogen gas. For example:

silver bromide $\xrightarrow{\text{light}}$ silver + bromine

$$2AgBr(s) \longrightarrow 2Ag(s) + Br_2(g)$$

The film now contains silver deposits of varying densities – depending on the amount of light which fell on the exposed film – and this forms a negative image. In other words, areas where lots of light fell have a heavier layer of silver (which appears black) than areas where not much light fell.

The silver halides don't just decompose in the presence of light. They are affected in the same way by X-rays and by the radiation from radioactive substances.

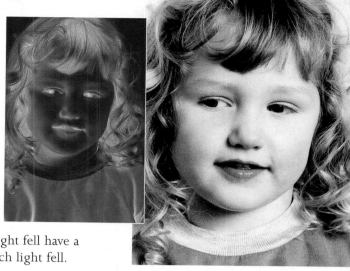

↗ **Figure 2:** The difference between a negative and the real appearance can clearly be seen here, with the heavy silver deposits in what are actually the lightest areas of the picture.

Ideas and Evidence

Silver halides, X-rays and radiation

In 1895 Wilhelm Röntgen discovered by accident that the silver halides are decomposed by X-rays, just as they are by light, and within three months X-ray photographs were being used by doctors to help diagnose and set broken bones.

Only a year after Röntgen had discovered X-rays, the Frenchman Antoine-Henri Becquerel tried to demonstrate that X-rays are produced by some chemicals after they are exposed to sunlight. He covered photographic plates with a thick layer of black paper to keep the light off them and placed a lump of uranium salt on top. After exposing the salt to the sunlight he developed the film and there was an image of the salt – made, he assumed, by X-rays. Becquerel set up more plates in the same way but the sun didn't shine so he put the plates in his desk drawer for several days. He then developed the photographic plate regardless, and was astonished to find a clear image of the salt. He had discovered radioactivity.

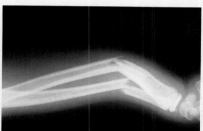

← **Figure 3:** X-rays depending on the decomposition of the silver halides are as important in medicine today as they were a hundred years ago for showing damage to bones.

← **Figure 4:** Antoine Becquerel discovered radioactivity in uranium through one of its properties – it affects photographic film, causing the silver bromide or iodide to decompose and the silver to be deposited to form a negative image.

Questions

1 a Produce an experimental procedure for making the transition metal salt of your choice, using a metal oxide or hydroxide and an acid.

  b Give one advantage of using insoluble compounds in a reaction like this.

  c Give one disadvantage of using insoluble compounds.

2 Explain how silver halides are used in photography.

Key Ideas

⊙ Salts of transition metals can be made by reacting their insoluble oxides or hydroxides with acids.

⊙ After reaction with the acid the excess metal oxide or hydroxide is filtered off.

⊙ Silver halides are reduced to silver by the action of light, X-rays and the radioactivity from radioactive substances.

⊙ Silver halides are used to make photographic film.

7.5 Sodium chloride – the best known salt

One salt is known to almost everyone because of its widespread use in everyday life. It is a compound of an alkali metal and a halogen, but sodium chloride is much better known simply as salt.

Salt has been important to people from the earliest times. It is actually vital for our health, and it is used around the world to enhance the flavour of food. The Romans valued it so highly that they were paid a certain amount of salt as part of their wages – the word salary comes from the Latin for salt, *salarium*. Salt is still of enormous importance in human life, not only as a seasoning and preservative for food, but as a major resource for the chemical industries.

Hundreds of thousands of tonnes of salt are used yearly around the world – but where does it all come from? One obvious source of salt is the oceans – sea water is salty. The other main source is in underground deposits – huge amounts of salt left behind millions of years ago when ancient seas evaporated as the climate changed.

↑ **Figure 1:** Sodium chloride (common salt) is an important factor in sea water, and in the cells of all the animals and plants that live either in the water or on the land above it.

← **Figure 2:** This vehicle is spraying rock salt – a mixture of salt, sand and grit – onto roads covered by ice and snow. The salt lowers the freezing point of water and so melts the ice, while the sand and grit provide more grip for car tyres.

How do we get salt?

In many of the hotter countries of the world salt is extracted from the oceans. The sea water is poured into big, flat open tanks and then the water evaporates away in the hot sun, leaving pure salt crystals behind. This method is even used on a very small scale in the UK, to produce high quality sea salt for eating, but the climate in the UK is simply not suitable for large scale salt production from the sea.

In many other countries, including the UK, salt is extracted from underground deposits. The salt is mined and brought to the surface in the form of rock salt, which is basically a mixture of sand and salt. Depending on the intended use, the pure salt may then have to be extracted, usually by dissolving it in water to make salt solution (known as brine).

↑ **Figure 3:** The salt extracted from these salt mines in Cheshire was once part of the sea water in a massive prehistoric sea.

Using the salt

Some of the salt extracted is used in the food production industry, while the rest is used for making chemicals. One very important industrial process is the electrolysis of sodium chloride solution (brine). Chlorine gas is formed at the positive electrode, hydrogen gas is formed at the negative electrode, and a solution of sodium hydroxide is also formed and collected:

sodium chloride + water $\longrightarrow$ hydrogen + chlorine + sodium hydroxide

These three products are all useful in different ways (see Section 7.6).

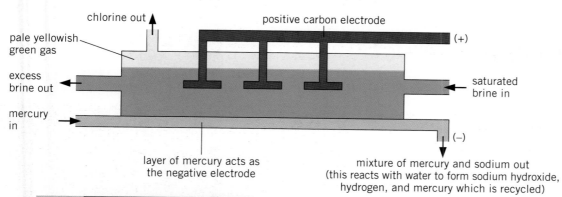

chlorine out

pale yellowish green gas

excess brine out

mercury in

positive carbon electrode (+)

saturated brine in

layer of mercury acts as the negative electrode

(−)

mixture of mercury and sodium out (this reacts with water to form sodium hydroxide, hydrogen, and mercury which is recycled)

← **Figure 4:** The industrial electrolysis of brine is an almost waste-free chemical process. All of the products are collected and are useful, and any spare brine is simply sent around again.

Ideas and Evidence

Making it pay

The chlorine, hydrogen and sodium hydroxide produced by the electrolysis of brine are known as **co-products**. The amounts of each chemical produced are always in the same proportions. The good thing about this reaction is that all the products are useful (see Section 7.6). The difficult thing is that you cannot make one of the products without also making the others, so any company which electrolyses sodium chloride needs to be sure that it can sell all of the products that will result, not just one or two of them! What is more, it is vital that the value of the products is substantially more than the cost of the raw materials, because the company has to pay for the chemical plant used, for the electricity to break down the sodium chloride and for the staff to look after the process. To be financially viable it has to do more than just cover these costs – it must make a profit as well.

↓ **Figure 5:** Although the costs of raw materials and the prices which can be charged for products change all the time, these figures give some idea of the balance of chemicals and costings in the electrolysis of brine.

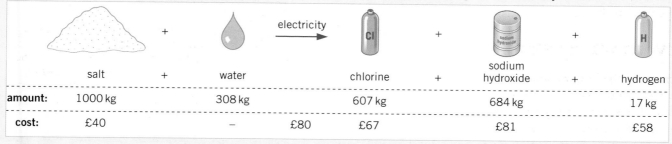

	salt	+	water	chlorine	+	sodium hydroxide	+	hydrogen
amount:	1000 kg		308 kg	607 kg		684 kg		17 kg
cost:	£40		− £80	£67		£81		£58

? Questions

1 a What are the two main sources of salt for the chemical and food industries?

b What are the advantages and disadvantages of the two methods of extraction?

2 Give a step-by-step description of the electrolysis of brine.

H 3 Give half equations for the reactions at the positive and negative electrodes in Figure 4.

4 Using the data in Figure 5, produce a pie chart to show the proportions of the different products of the electrolysis of brine.

H 5 If 117 g of sodium chloride were used in an electrolysis experiment, what mass of chlorine, sodium hydroxide and hydrogen would you expect to be produced?

🔑 Key Ideas

⊙ Sodium chloride (common salt) is found in large quantities in the sea and in underground deposits.

⊙ The electrolysis of sodium chloride solution (brine) is an important industrial process.

⊙ The products of the electrolysis are chlorine gas at the positive electrode, hydrogen gas at the negative electrode and sodium hydroxide in the tank.

7.6 Using brine products

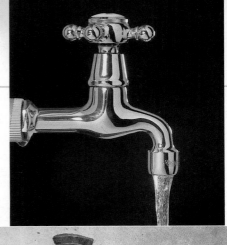

The electrolysis of brine results in chlorine, hydrogen and sodium hydroxide. All of these products are useful in their own right and some of them can be reacted together to make yet more useful products.

Chlorine

We know that chlorine is a poisonous green gas which bleaches damp litmus paper in the laboratory and causes great damage to the human body if it is inhaled in even tiny quantities. But it is also a tremendously useful chemical, both on its own and in combination with other elements. The chlorine produced by the electrolysis of brine plays a vital role in public health, because it is used to kill bacteria in drinking water and in swimming pools.

The chlorine may also be reacted with the sodium hydroxide produced in the electrolysis of brine to produce bleach (sodium chlorate(I)). Bleach is a strong oxidising agent which is very good at killing bacteria, and it is used extensively in homes, hospitals and industry to maintain hygienic conditions. Chlorine is also used in the manufacture of many other disinfectants, hydrochloric acid and the plastic (polymer) known as PVC.

Hydrogen

Hydrogen is a potentially explosive gas, yet once it has been produced, collected and stored in cylinders under pressure it has many important industrial uses. The Haber process for the production of ammonia (see Sections 4.8 and 9.6) depends on a ready supply of hydrogen. The manufacture of margarine involves bubbling hydrogen through vegetable oils under different conditions and in the presence of a catalyst to turn the oil into a soft spreadable solid. Finally hydrogen can be reacted with the chlorine also made by the electrolysis of brine to make hydrogen chloride which is then reacted with water to give hydrochloric acid. The acid made in this way is particularly pure and so it is widely used in the food and pharmaceutical industries.

↑ **Figure 1:** Chlorine is a chemical which has been put to terribly destructive use as a poisonous gas during wartime, yet it brings us clean, disease-free drinking water and keeps our homes, schools, industries and hospitals relatively free from infectious bacteria.

↓ **Figure 2:** Hydrogen is needed to make the vast amounts of margarine eaten every day all around the world. It is reacted with vegetable oils in equipment like this.

Sodium hydroxide

The sodium hydroxide which is left after the electrolysis of brine has to be purified because it is mixed with any remaining brine. Once that is done it is used for a variety of processes which include the manufacture of soap, paper and ceramics. Oven cleaners are based on sodium hydroxide too. The other major use of sodium hydroxide is to combine it with the chlorine produced to make bleach (see above).

A common way of increasing the rate of chemical reactions is to increase the **concentration** of the reactants. (Obviously this only applies if the reactants are in solution!) Similarly, if the reactants are gases, increasing the **pressure** at which they are reacting has the same effect.

If a solution is more concentrated it will have more particles of the reactants moving around in it. The more 'crowded' the reactant particles are, the more likely it is that they will bump into each other and a reaction will take place. In the same way, increasing the pressure of a mixture of gases squashes the gaseous particles more closely together. This increases the chance that they will collide and react, and so speeds up the rate of the reaction.

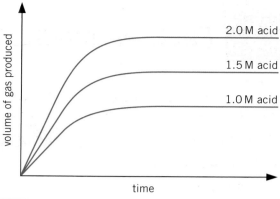

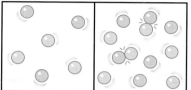

low concentration/ high concentration/
low pressure   high pressure

↖ **Figure 4:** The rate of reaction between calcium carbonate and sulphuric acid increases as concentration increases because the rate at which particles collide increases.

? **Questions**

1 The data in this table is from a reaction carried out at two different temperatures:

Time of reading (minutes)	Total volume of gas given off at 30 °C (cm³)	Total volume of gas given off at 40 °C (cm³)
1	5	10
2	10	20
3	15	30
4	20	40
5	25	40
6	30	40
7	35	40
8	40	40
9	40	40

a Draw a graph of this data, plotting time along the x-axis.

b What does this data tell you about the effect of temperature on the rate of a reaction?

c Explain how temperature affects the rate of a reaction like this one.

2 Acid toilet cleaners designed to remove lime scale work better if they are used neat than if they are diluted with water. Explain why, using ideas about collision theory in your answer.

3 How does increasing the pressure of a gas mixture have the same effect on the rate of a reaction as increasing the concentration of reactants in solution?

4 Use your chemical knowledge to explain why acid rain damage on marble statues has increased significantly in the last few years.

Key Ideas

⊙ The rate of a chemical reaction increases if the temperature increases.

⊙ The rate of a chemical reaction increases if the concentration of dissolved reactants increases or if the pressure of gaseous reactants increases.

⊙ Increasing the temperature increases the speed of reacting particles so they collide more frequently and more energetically.

⊙ Increasing the concentration or pressure increases the frequency of collisions between reacting particles.

⊙ The minimum amount of energy that particles must have in order to react is known as the activation energy.

8.3 More about reaction rates

We can increase the rate of a chemical reaction by increasing the temperature or the effective concentration of the reacting particles, but there are other ways of changing reaction rates as well.

Increasing surface area

When you eat a piece of food, you chew it to break it up into small pieces – you don't usually swallow it whole, even though this would get it into your stomach more quickly! Digesting food is a chemical reaction, so by doing this you are controlling the rate of reaction.

If you want to boil potatoes quickly, you can cut them up into small pieces first. Cooking is a chemical reaction, so by doing this you are controlling the rate of reaction. Similarly, if you are trying to light a fire, you don't pile large logs together and try to set them alight – you use small pieces of kindling to begin with and then add the larger pieces of wood later, once the fire is going.

When a solid reactant is involved in a chemical reaction with a solution, the size of the pieces of the solid material make a big difference to the speed of the reaction. The inside of a large lump of a chemical is not in contact with the solution it is reacting with, so it can't react – it has to wait for the outside to react first. In smaller lumps or in a powder each grain is surrounded by solution and so reactions can take place easily.

↑ **Figure 1:** Without small pieces of kindling to get it going, a roaring fire like this would be almost impossible.

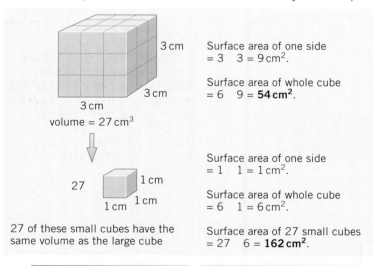

3 cm
3 cm
3 cm
volume = 27 cm³

Surface area of one side
= 3 × 3 = 9 cm².

Surface area of whole cube
= 6 × 9 = **54 cm²**.

27

1 cm
1 cm
1 cm

Surface area of one side
= 1 × 1 = 1 cm².

Surface area of whole cube
= 6 × 1 = 6 cm².

27 of these small cubes have the same volume as the large cube

Surface area of 27 small cubes
= 27 × 6 = **162 cm²**.

↑ **Figure 2:** When a solid reacts, the size of the pieces of it make a big difference to the rate of the reaction – the smaller the pieces, the faster the reaction. This is shown very clearly when equal masses of magnesium ribbon and magnesium powder are added to 250 cm³ of 1 molar HCl!

↑ **Figure 3:** Although flour seems harmless enough, it can react rapidly with air if the particles of flour are small enough. This flour mill in London was wrecked when flour dust caused a violent explosion.

For centuries people knew that sugar was needed for the formation of alcoholic drinks, but they thought that the sugar simply broke down to form alcohol. They did not know that wild yeasts were already present on the skins of the grapes (or other fruits being fermented) so yeast did not need to be added separately. Louis Pasteur knew that although sugar is an optically active molecule (it rotates polarised light), when it breaks down the optical activity is lost. Yet in the 1850s Pasteur showed that a fermented mixture was optically active. He knew that (at that time) only living organisms were capable of creating new molecules which affected polarised light. So he reasoned that fermentation must be a process involving living organisms – the yeast cells he found in the brews. If people provided the living yeast with ideal conditions to grow, brewing and wine-making could move from small scale operations to larger factory-based operations. This is exactly what happened, and now specific types of yeast are added to produce reliable and distinctive products.

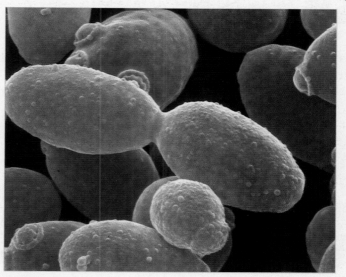

↑ **Figure 4:** This micrograph shows yeast cells, magnified over 4000 times. It was Louis Pasteur who first recognised the role of yeast in the production of alcohol, paving the way for a major change in the management of brewing beer and wine-making.

Enzymes and milk

Sometimes milk 'goes off' as a result of the action of bacteria, and it looks, tastes and smells disgusting. At other times we actually want our milk to go off – but in the way and at the speed we choose. Yoghurt and cheese are the result of milk that has gone off in very controlled conditions. In yoghurt making, specific bacteria are allowed to grow in milk which has been pasteurised (heat treated) to get rid of the unwanted bacteria which would otherwise give it an unpleasant taste and smell. The mixture of milk and bacteria is kept at a temperature of around 45 °C and the yoghurt-making bacteria convert **lactose**, the natural sugar found in milk, to **lactic acid**, the chemical which gives yoghurts their slightly sharp taste. Cheese making is very similar, except that the bacteria and milk are kept at much lower temperatures and only the solid curds produced are used to make the cheese.

1 Explain why enzymes are so important and give three examples of their use in the food industry.

2 Explain the importance of the work of Louis Pasteur in developing our understanding of the fermentation process and of enzymes.

3 Produce an information leaflet on one of the following industries, explaining the processes by which the product is made:

   brewing/wine-making

   the baking industry

   yoghurt production.

   The leaflet is to be used with pupils in years 6 and 7.

⊙ Living cells use chemical reactions to produce new materials.

⊙ In fermentation, yeast cells convert sugar to carbon dioxide and alcohol (ethanol).

⊙ Carbon dioxide turns limewater cloudy.

⊙ Milk is turned into yoghurt by the action of bacteria which convert lactose to lactic acid.

Since the end of the 19th century, when enzymes were first isolated from living cells, we have found more and more ways of using enzymes in industry. The application of this new science is an example of biotechnology.

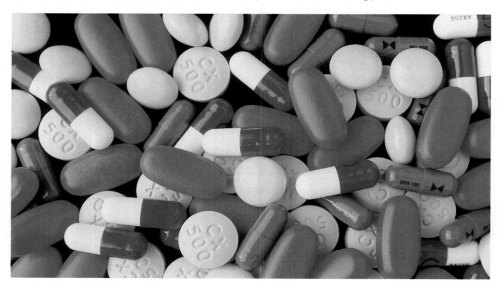

← **Figure 1:** A surprising number of the medicines we take, including the important antibiotic penicillin, are made using enzymes supplied by microorganisms.

Advantages and disadvantages of enzymes

In a chemical industrial process, one of the main problems is getting the reactions to happen at relatively normal temperatures and pressures. Constantly supplying heat, and building plants that can withstand high pressures, require expensive and energy-demanding equipment. So there is a constant quest for ways of carrying out reactions under relatively normal conditions. Enzymes can provide the perfect answer, safely catalysing reactions so that they occur at relatively low temperatures and pressures.

The main problem with using enzymes is that they are very sensitive to their surroundings (see Section 8.4). For enzymes to function properly the temperature must be kept down, below around 45 °C, and the pH also needs to be kept within closely monitored limits which suit the particular enzyme.

Enzymes are used industrially in two main ways. Some processes use the whole microorganism to provide the enzyme. These include brewing and the production of antibiotics like penicillin. However, whole microorganisms use up a lot of the substrate simply making new microorganisms, so some industrial processes use *pure* enzymes – enzymes which have been isolated from the microorganisms in which they were made. Pure enzymes use the substrate much more efficiently, although they are more expensive to produce.

What are enzymes used for?

The number of different uses for microorganisms and the enzymes they produce is growing all the time. The production of human insulin by enzymes in genetically engineered bacteria is one example of a relatively new use of whole microorganisms in biotechnology.

Pure enzymes (such as proteases, carbohydrases and isomerase) have many uses too. **Proteases** (protein digesting enzymes) are used in the manufacture of baby foods. They 'pre-digest' some of the protein, making it easier for a baby's digestive system to cope with.

Carbohydrases (carbohydrate digesting enzymes) are used to convert starch syrup into sugar (glucose) syrup. Huge quantities of sugar syrup are used in food production – just look at the ingredients labels of all sorts of foods. Using enzymes to convert plant starch into sweet sugar provides a cheap source of sweetness for food manufacturers. It is also important in the process of making fuel from plants such as maize.

Sometimes the glucose syrup made from starch is passed into another process using a different set of enzymes. **Isomerase** is used to convert glucose syrup into fructose syrup, by rearranging the atoms within the glucose molecule. The fructose syrup is much sweeter than glucose, and therefore smaller amounts of it are needed to make food taste sweet. As a result, fructose is widely used to sweeten 'slimming' foods – the food tastes sweet yet contains fewer calories.

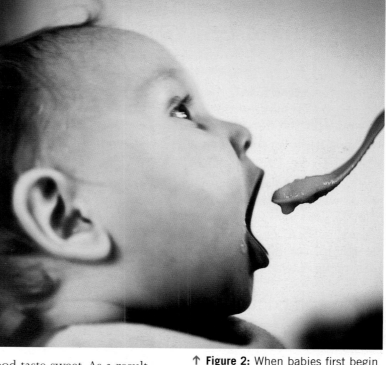

↑ **Figure 2:** When babies first begin to eat solid foods they are not very good at it. They may be given foods containing protein which has been pre-digested by enzymes, so it is easier for them to extract the goodness they need from their food.

Some uses of enzymes are very mundane – for example in biological detergents. The detergents contain proteases and **lipases** (fat digesting enzymes) which break down the proteins and fats in the dirt we get on our clothes – and so help provide a cleaner wash.

← **Figure 3:** Millions of people in the UK, the US and around the world are overweight – and many of them are trying to slim. The market for slimming foods is enormous – and so more and more glucose syrup is converted to fructose syrup using enzyme technology.

? Questions

1 Make a table to show the advantages and disadvantages of using enzymes as catalysts to bring about chemical reactions in an industrial process.

2 Why are pure enzymes sometimes used instead of whole microorganisms in industrial processes?

3 Biological washing powders contain enzymes in tiny capsules. Explain why they are more effective than ordinary washing powders at lower temperatures.

4 Carry out a survey of the 'ingredients' labels of a number of different foods. Find how many foods in your sample contain sugar or glucose syrup and how many contain fructose syrup. Show your results graphically in some way.

⊙ Key Ideas

⊙ Enzymes are used in industry to bring about reactions at normal temperatures and pressure that would otherwise require expensive, energy-demanding equipment.

⊙ Whole microorganisms or pure enzymes may be used in industrial processes.

⊙ Enzymes are used in a wide range of different processes including the manufacture of baby foods, producing sugar from starch, producing slimming foods, as biological detergents and for making antibiotics and human insulin.

Using enzymes successfully

Industrial processes based on enzymes as catalysts may use whole microorganisms in the process or they may use pure, isolated enzymes extracted from microorganisms. Whichever method is used, care has to be taken to ensure that the enzymes work as effectively and economically as possible.

When the whole microorganism is used, a successful industrial process will depend on stabilising the organism and maintaining optimum conditions for its growth and survival, so that it keeps on functioning for as long as possible. The temperature must be correct, the right balance of nutrients supplied, oxygen levels maintained, and waste products removed if possible to control the pH levels.

Batch and continuous processes

Industrial processes using microorganisms usually operate either a **batch** process or a **continuous** process. In a batch process the microorganisms are cultured with a fixed volume of food medium, and they grow and use up the nutrients until they have reached a maximum population and have manufactured lots of the desired product. At this stage the whole process is halted, since the rate at which the products are produced starts to slow down as the nutrients run out. The products (often antibiotics or enzymes for another process) are then harvested and the culture tanks cleaned and sterilised before a new batch culture is started up.

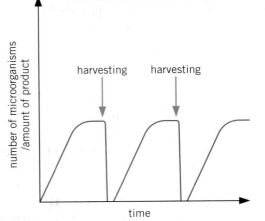

→ **Figure 1:** The manufacture of penicillin, which takes place in an enormous chemical plant like the one above, is an example of batch culture. The graph shows the typical pattern for this type of process.

Science people

The penicillin story

In 1928 Alexander Fleming noticed that a mould which had grown accidentally on a culture of bacteria had stopped them growing. Eleven years later Howard Florey and Ernst Chain managed to develop the antibiotic penicillin from penicillium mould, but it was virtually impossible to extract enough of the drug from the mould to cure patients on a large scale.

With the onset of the Second World War, the need for penicillin became even more urgent with the casualties on the battlefield. But mass production of the miraculous-seeming drug was not possible until several big American pharmaceutical companies stepped in with huge fermentation plants which they had developed for other processes. These plants, combined with the lucky discovery of another type of penicillin mould (found by one of the scientists on a mouldy melon in a market!) which gave a much higher yield of penicillin drug than the original type, meant that large scale production of the antibiotic began in earnest, saving the lives of millions of soldiers and civilians in the years that followed.

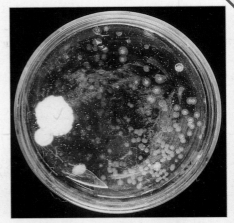

↑ **Figure 2:** The realisation that a chemical compound made by a mould could destroy bacteria – seen here on Fleming's original plate – led eventually to the development of antibiotics, drugs which still save millions of lives every year.

In a continuous process extra nutrients are added at regular intervals during the growth of the colony of microorganisms. At the same time some of the products along with microorganisms and wastes are removed, so the volume within the system stays the same. Continuous production is used for making single-celled protein (sold as Quorn ™) and in some forms of waste-water treatment. This system has many advantages, not least because it allows for production without breaks for cleaning and setting up new cultures, but batch production has other advantages – it is more flexible if demand is variable, and it is less prone to contamination. With the increasing use of pure enzymes more continuous processes are being developed, because the growth of the microorganisms is no longer a factor and so a much better yield is obtained.

Using pure enzymes

Increasingly scientists are looking at using isolated pure enzymes in industrial processes instead of whole microorganisms. This has lots of advantages – for example, all of the substrate provided will be converted into product (whereas whole microorganisms use a lot of substrate just for growing new microorganism), and ideal conditions for the specific enzyme can be used. What is more, only one pure product is formed because each enzyme only catalyses one reaction.

However, using pure enzymes can be very wasteful. They are quite expensive to produce, yet at the end of the process when the products are harvested, they cannot usually be recovered and so they are simply lost. This is why the newest areas of enzyme technology are involved in developing *immobilised* enzymes. The enzymes are immobilised (trapped and held) in an inert solid which does not interfere with their catalytic action. This holds them stationary while they catalyse the desired reaction. The enzymes can then be recovered from the reaction mixture at the end of the process and reused time after time. This makes the whole process more economical, much easier to control, and also means that the enzymes do not contaminate the end product.

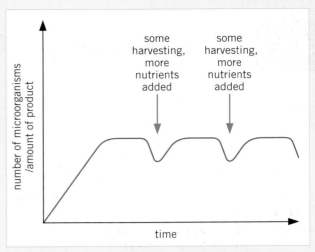

↑ **Figure 3:** Continuous culture is an ideal situation – but it does not give the best results with all microorganisms.

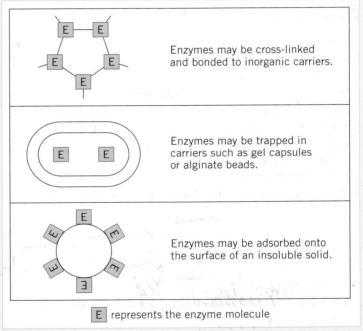

Enzymes may be cross-linked and bonded to inorganic carriers.

Enzymes may be trapped in carriers such as gel capsules or alginate beads.

Enzymes may be adsorbed onto the surface of an insoluble solid.

E represents the enzyme molecule

↑ **Figure 4:** Immobilised enzymes can be used time and time again. The enzymes may be trapped in a solid sheet or in a carrier such as inert alginate beads (made from an extract of seaweed).

1 a Indigestion tablets called **antacids** can be taken to react with excess hydrochloric acid in the stomach. A student investigated two different antacid tablets labelled **X** and **Y**.

Both tablets **X** and **Y** contained calcium carbonate.

  i Calculate the formula mass (M_r) of calcium carbonate, $CaCO_3$.
(Relative atomic masses: Ca = 40, C = 12, O = 16)   **(2 marks)**

  ii Name the gas formed when calcium carbonate reacts with hydrochloric acid.
        (1 mark)

b The student first reacted tablet **X**, and then tablet **Y**, with 100 cm³ of a hydrochloric acid solution. The student measured the volume of gas produced during the first five minutes. The results are shown in the table.

Time in minutes	Volume of gas in cm³ Tablet X	Volume of gas in cm³ Tablet Y
0	0	0
1	38	31
2	48	54
3	48	67
4	48	72
5	48	72

  i Draw a graph of the results for tablet **Y**.
(A graph of the results for tablet **X** has been drawn for you. Copy it onto your graph for tablet **Y**.)   **(3 marks)**

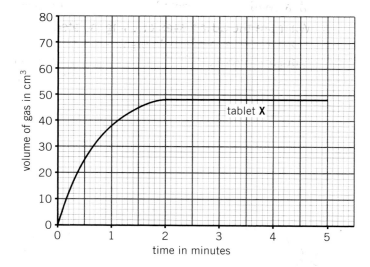

ii Tablet **X** contains less calcium carbonate than tablet **Y**.
How do the results show this?   **(1 mark)**

iii Explain why the rate of reaction slows down for both tablets.   **(2 marks)**
(Total 9 marks)
AQA specimen question

2 a What are enzymes?   **(1 mark)**

b Explain why enzymes are used in industry.
   (3 marks)
(Total 4 marks)
AQA specimen question

3 The drawing shows a reaction carried out by a student.

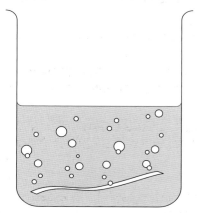

The experiment involved reacting a piece of magnesium ribbon with 1 M sulphuric acid.

a Suggest **one** way in which the student could measure the rate at which this reaction takes place.   **(1 mark)**

b Suggest **three** ways in which the student could increase the rate of the reaction.   **(3 marks)**

c Explain how each of these methods has its effect on the rate of the reaction.   **(6 marks)**
(Total 10 marks)

4 The following data shows the results obtained by two students when they reacted the same mass of calcium carbonate with 0.5 M acid. In one reaction the calcium carbonate was kept in lumps, in the other it was ground to a powder.

Time of reading in minutes	Total volume of gas given off in cm³ (lumps of calcium carbonate)	Total volume of gas given off in cm³ (powdered calcium carbonate)
1	5	15
2	10	30
3	15	40
4	20	43
5	25	45
6	30	45
7	35	45
8	40	45
9	43	45
10	45	45
11	45	45

a Plot a graph of these results, with time on the *x*-axis. (4 marks)

b What do these results show about the effect of surface area on reaction rate? (1 mark)

c Why does the surface area of a solid reactant have such an effect on the rate of a reaction? (2 marks)

d Although the rates of the two reactions were different, the total amount of gas produced was the same. Why? (1 mark)

(Total 8 marks)

5 The use of enzymes in industrial processes is increasing all the time.

a What is an enzyme? (1 mark)

Use the information in the diagram to help you answer the rest of this question.

The diagram shows a graph of the rate of an enzyme-controlled reaction at different temperatures.

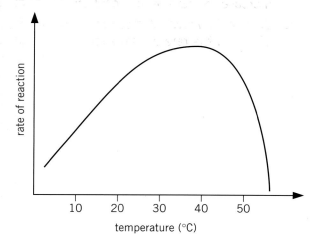

b At what temperature is this enzyme most effective? (1 mark)

c **i** What happens to the level of enzyme activity after 50 °C? (1 mark)

ii Why does this happen? (2 marks)

d The pH of the reacting mixture also affects the rate of an enzyme-controlled reaction. Explain why. (2 marks)

(Total 7 marks)

H 6 a When whole microorganisms are used in an industrial process they are grown in large fermenters like this one.

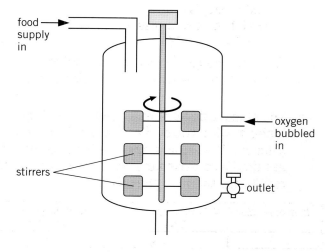

Explain the importance of:
i the food supply (1 mark)
ii the oxygen supply (1 mark)
iii the stirrers. (1 mark)

b Industrial processes using microorganisms are usually run either as **batch** processes or **continuous** processes. What is meant by:
i a batch process (2 marks)
ii a continuous process? (2 marks)

c What are the advantages of using isolated enzymes instead of whole organisms in industrial processes? (2 marks)

(Total 9 marks)

9.1 Energy in reactions

Whenever chemical reactions take place energy is involved, as chemical bonds are broken and formed. Energy is usually transferred either to or from the surroundings.

⊙ Reactions which transfer energy, often as heat, to the surroundings are known as **exothermic reactions** and we can measure a rise in temperature as the reaction progresses.

⊙ On the other hand, reactions which transfer energy, again often as heat, from the surroundings to the reacting chemicals are known as **endothermic reactions** and we can measure a drop in temperature as the reaction progresses.

Exothermic reactions

← **Figure 1:** When a fuel like this wood burns in oxygen we get a very clear illustration of what is meant by an exothermic reaction – we don't need a thermometer to measure the temperature change!

Fuels burning are a clear example of exothermic reactions, but there are a number of others which we often meet in the laboratory. Neutralisation reactions between acids and alkalis are exothermic, and the rise in temperature can easily be measured. Similarly the addition of water to white anhydrous copper(II) sulphate (anhydrous means 'without water') produces blue hydrated copper(II) sulphate crystals and heat – another exothermic reaction.

Respiration is a very special form of burning fuel. It involves the burning of sugar with oxygen, within the cells of every living organism, to produce the energy needed for all the reactions of life along with water and carbon dioxide as waste products. Respiration is another exothermic reaction.

↑ **Figure 2:** Warm-blooded animals such as this harvest mouse – and humans – depend on the heat generated by exothermic respiration to maintain the body temperature at a constant level, regardless of the weather.

Endothermic reactions

Endothermic reactions are less common than exothermic ones, but there are a number which are quite familiar. For example, when certain salts such as potassium chloride and ammonium nitrate dissolve in water they take in heat from the surroundings and the temperature of the solution drops. Also, any thermal decomposition reaction is endothermic, because the reaction only takes place if heat is put into the system. The breakdown of calcium carbonate to calcium oxide and carbon dioxide is one example – the reaction only takes place if the calcium carbonate is heated up to 800 °C, so the reaction takes in a great deal of energy from the surroundings. Another enormously important endothermic reaction is photosynthesis. Photosynthesis is the reaction by which plants turn carbon dioxide and water into sugar and oxygen, using energy from the sun.

↑ **Figure 3:** Sherbet dissolving in water is an endothermic reaction – the slight cooling sensation on the tongue adds to the fizzy sour effect of these sweets.

← **Figure 4:** Photosynthesis takes place in the green parts of plants all over the world – it is probably the most common endothermic reaction on Earth.

0–ᴍ Key Ideas

⊙ When chemical reactions occur energy is usually transferred to or from the surroundings.

⊙ An exothermic reaction transfers energy to the surroundings.

⊙ An endothermic reaction takes in energy from the surroundings.

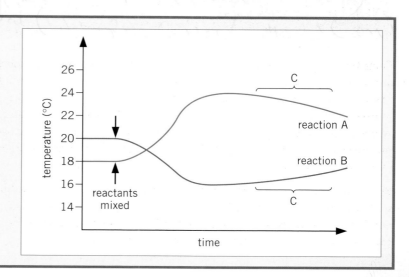

During any chemical reaction, existing chemical bonds are broken and new bonds are formed. Energy has to be supplied to break chemical bonds, so breaking bonds is an endothermic process – energy is taken in. However, when new bonds are formed, energy is released, so bond formation is an exothermic process.

In an exothermic reaction the energy released when new bonds are formed is greater than the energy used in breaking existing bonds, so overall energy is transferred from the reaction into the surroundings, usually meaning heat is given out.

In an endothermic reaction the energy required to break existing bonds is greater than the energy released when new bonds are formed, so overall energy is transferred from the surroundings to the reacting chemicals, usually meaning heat is taken in.

It is the *balance* between the energy which must be supplied to break existing bonds and the energy which is released when new bonds are formed, which determines whether a reaction is endothermic or exothermic. We can find out more about what is happening in a particular reaction by looking at energy level diagrams.

Energy level diagrams

Energy level diagrams show us the relative energy contained in the molecules of the reactants and the products of a reaction. This energy is expressed in kJ/mole – it represents the energy needed to make or break the bonds within 1 mole of the chemical elements or compounds involved in the reaction.

Diagrams like Figure 1 show us three different, important things.

⊙ This is an exothermic reaction – the products are at a lower energy level than the reactants, so energy has been given out in the reaction.

⊙ The difference between the energy of the reactants and the products indicates the amount of energy given out during the reaction (per mole). In an exothermic reaction, because the products contain less energy than the reactants, this number is always *negative*. This difference in energy between the reactants and the products is shown as **ΔH**, so we can say that in an exothermic reaction ΔH will always be negative.

⊙ Thirdly, we can see that to begin with, the energy line rises higher than the energy of the reactants. This represents the energy which has to be put into the reaction initially to break the existing bonds. This is the **activation energy** which has to be supplied before the reaction takes place at all.

In an energy level diagram for an endothermic reaction (Figure 2) we can see that the situation is reversed. The products are at a higher energy level than the reactants. This means that the difference between the energy levels (ΔH) is positive. The difference in the height represents the energy taken in during the reaction. As in Figure 1, the energy line goes higher than the level of the products, representing the energy needed to break down the existing bonds – again this is the activation energy.

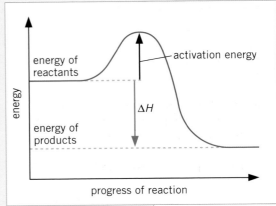

↑ **Figure 1:** This is a typical energy level diagram for an exothermic reaction.

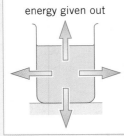

↓ **Figure 2:** This is a typical energy level diagram for an endothermic reaction.

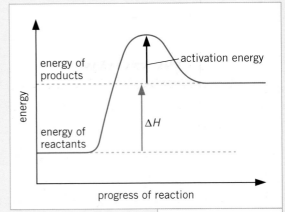

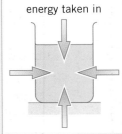

Energy transfers in practice

We can look at some energy level diagrams for real reactions and see what they have to tell us.

Example 1

Sodium and chlorine react together violently to give sodium chloride. Is this a reaction where energy is taken in or given out?

As we can see from Figure 3, the products have much less energy than the reactants. ΔH is strongly negative, so we can tell that the reaction between sodium and chlorine is strongly exothermic.

Example 2

Solid ammonium chloride dissolves in water. The energy level diagram for the reaction is shown Figure 4.

In this case the diagram shows us that when ammonium chloride dissolves in water the energy of the products is higher than that of the reactants. ΔH is positive and the reaction is endothermic.

ammonium chloride solution

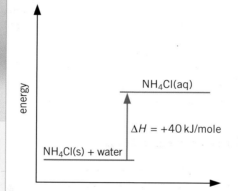

→ **Figure 4:** Energy level diagram for the formation of ammonium chloride solution.

sodium chloride crystals

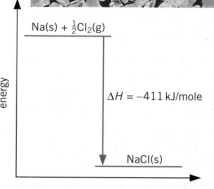

↑ **Figure 3:** Energy level diagram for the formation of sodium chloride.

Questions

1 Sketch energy level diagrams for the following reactions:

  a $6CO_2 + 6H_2O \longrightarrow C_6H_{12}O_6 + 6O_2$ ΔH = +2880 kJ/mole

  b $C + O_2 \longrightarrow CO_2$ ΔH = −394 kJ/mole

  c $H_2 + I_2 \longrightarrow 2HI$ ΔH = + 26.5 kJ/mole

  d $C_5H_{12} + 8O_2 \longrightarrow 5CO_2 + 6H_2O$ ΔH = −3500 kJ/mole

2 **a** During all chemical reactions energy needs to be supplied for the reaction to take place. Why?

  b At some point during all chemical reactions some energy is released – when?

  c Explain how the balance of the energy taken in and given out affects the type of reaction taking place.

The activation energy is the minimum amount of energy needed by the reacting particles in any particular reaction for that reaction to take place. Unless particles collide with sufficient energy to supply the activation energy they simply don't react. The activation energy must be supplied before a reaction can take place. For example, when fireworks explode a strongly exothermic reaction is taking place, yet the chemicals which react so violently sit harmlessly in the cardboard tube until we 'light the blue touch paper and retire'! The heat from the burning of the blue fuse paper supplies the activation energy needed to start the reaction of the chemicals in the tube.

The activation energy needed for a reaction to take place is quite separate from the energy difference between the reactants and the products (ΔH). This is why even exothermic reactions often need heating to get them started.

The catalyst contribution

Catalysts are extremely important in the laboratory and particularly in the chemical industries because they speed up the rate of a reaction (see Section 8.3). Catalysts speed up the rate of reactions by lowering the activation energy needed for each reaction to take place. This means that many more of the collisions which occur between reacting particles actually result in a reaction taking place, and this in turn results in an increased reaction rate. A catalyst effectively makes it easier for the reactants to react together and form the product.

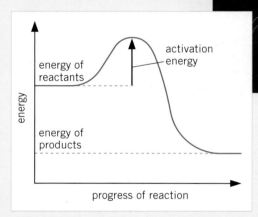

Figure 1: The spectacular chemistry of a firework display is stored safely until the activation energy is supplied by lighting the fuse.

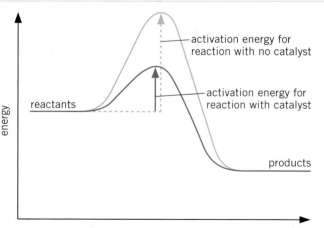

Figure 2: A catalyst has its effect by lowering the activation energy, making it easier for the reaction to take place and so speeding up the rate.

Whatever effect the catalyst has on lowering the activation energy of a reaction, the overall energy change (ΔH) remains the same. Enzymes, the biological catalysts which are so important in living cells and increasingly in industrial processes, work on the same principle of lowering the activation energy of the reaction which they catalyse.

Nanotechnology and catalysis

The use of catalysts and enzymes has been increasingly developed over the last century. So far most of the uses have involved speeding up industrial reactions to make them faster and more economic. Catalysts are also being used in an attempt to 'clean up' some of our modern technology, helping to reduce the pollution from car exhausts in catalytic converters.

Some new and quite mind-boggling uses of catalysts and enzymes are beginning to emerge from science laboratories around the world. For example, there is an enzyme called ATPase, which releases the energy stored in a molecule called ATP and makes it available to cells – it is vital for all the reactions of life. Scientists have isolated this enzyme and used it to create a nanomotor. (*Nanotechnology* is the science of building tiny machines no bigger than 100 nanometres in size – 100 nanometres is one ten-thousandth of a millimetre.) They have fixed one end of the enzyme to a sheet of metal a few atoms thick, and attached a microscopic propeller to the other end of the enzyme molecule. When supplied with ATP, the enzyme catalyses the breakdown of ATP and the energy released is used to turn the propeller. These minute 'motors' are so powerful that, if they were the size of a human being, they would be able to rotate a propeller 1 km long even if it was in water! When the enzymes are flooded with ATP the propellers turn, and when the ATP runs out they stop. More ATP starts them up again. Because ATP is found naturally in cells this development is seen as a step towards biomachines, where in the future the join between biological systems and mechanical devices may be completely undetectable.

↑ **Figure 3:** Enzymes trapped in microscopic capsules like this speed up the process of getting our clothes clean when they are used in biological washing powders. Some of these capsules are open to reveal the enzymes within.

1 In any chemical reaction energy has to be supplied to make the reaction happen.

  a What is this energy needed for?

  b What is it called?

2 Explain why:

  a a high activation energy means a chemical reaction takes place slowly

  b a low activation energy means a chemical reaction tends to take place fast.

3 Catalysts speed up the rate of chemical reactions without being changed themselves. They are often found as very small beads or pellets with holes in them. Use your knowledge of chemical reactions and the factors affecting the rate of those reactions to answer the following questions.

  a How do catalysts increase the rate of chemical reactions?

  b Why are catalysts usually found as tiny beads or pellets with holes in them?

⊙ The activation energy is the minimum energy needed by reacting particles for a reaction to occur.

⊙ Catalysts have their effect by lowering the activation energy, making it easier for a reaction to take place and so speeding up the rate of a reaction

Bond energies

We don't actually need to carry out reactions and measure the energy changes which take place to decide whether the reaction is endothermic or exothermic. Every single type of chemical bond has a particular bond energy associated with it, and this allows us to calculate exactly how much energy will be taken in and released in a particular reaction.

The bond energy for a particular type of bond is always the same, no matter which compound it is found in. The bond energy is measured in kJ/mole. This represents the amount of energy in kilojoules needed to break 1 mole of that particular type of bond.

We can use known bond energies to work out the overall energy change in almost any reaction. To do this we need to have a list of the bond energies of some of the most commonly found chemical bonds. (The list is shown in the table.)

Working things out

To calculate the energy change in a reaction we need to work out how much energy is needed to break the existing bonds in the reactants, and then how much energy is released on the formation of the new bonds in the products.

It is very important to remember that the data in the table is the energy required for **breaking** bonds. Energy is taken in and the measurement is positive. However when we want to know the amount of energy released when those same bonds are **formed**, although the figure is the same, the sign is reversed. For example, the bond energy for the breaking of a carbon–carbon bond is +347 kJ/mole, and the bond energy for forming a C–C bond is −347 kJ/mole.

Example 1

When hydrogen and chlorine react together they form hydrogen chloride. We can work out the energy changes as follows.

⊙ First we need to know the balanced equation for the reaction:

$$H_2 + Cl_2 \longrightarrow 2HCl$$

⊙ This tells us that 1 mole of hydrogen molecules react with 1 mole of chlorine molecules to form 2 moles of hydrogen chloride molecules.

⊙ From our table of data we know that the energy needed to break apart 1 mole of hydrogen molecules (H–H bonds) is 436 kJ/mole, and the energy needed to break 1 mole of chlorine molecules (Cl–Cl bonds) is 242 kJ/mole. So the energy needed to break existing bonds in the reactants is:

$$436 + 242 = +678 \text{ kJ/mole}$$

glucose

methane

C — H
413 kJ/mole

CH₂OH

methane

glucose

↖ **Figure 1:** Whether it is part of a small methane molecule or a larger glucose molecule, the average bond energy of the carbon–hydrogen bond is 413 kJ/mole.

Bond	Bond energy (kJ/mole)
C–C	347
C–O	358
C–H	413
C–N	286
C–F	467
C–Cl	346
Cl–Cl	242
H–Cl	431
H–O	463
H–N	388
H–H	436

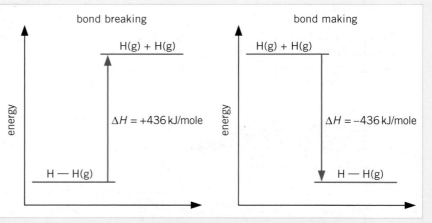

bond breaking

H(g) + H(g)

energy

$\Delta H = +436$ kJ/mole

H — H(g)

bond making

H(g) + H(g)

energy

$\Delta H = -436$ kJ/mole

H — H(g)

↑ **Figure 2:** The diagrams show the difference between the energy needed for the breaking and making of the same bond.

- From our table of data we also know how much energy will be released in the formation of 2 moles of hydrogen chloride (H–Cl bonds). As bonds are being formed, energy is released. So to form two moles of H–Cl the bond energy will be:

$$2 \times (-431)\,\text{kJ/mole} = -862\,\text{kJ/mole}$$

- To find the net energy transfer (overall energy change) for the reaction we combine the amount of energy taken in to break the bonds and the amount of energy released in bond formation:

$$\begin{array}{ccc}
\text{energy taken in} & + & \text{energy released} & = & \text{total energy transfer} \\
\text{during bond breaking} & & \text{during bond formation} & & \text{during the reaction} \\
678 & + & (-862) & = & -184\,\text{kJ/mole}
\end{array}$$

or $\Delta H = -184\,\text{kJ/mole}$

The negative number shows that more energy was released in bond formation than was needed to break existing bonds, telling us that the reaction is **exothermic**.

↑ **Figure 3:** We don't need calculations to tell us that some reactions – like the dynamite exploding inside this building – are exothermic!

Example 2

When steam is blown through white hot coke, the carbon is oxidised to carbon monoxide.

- The balanced equation for the reaction is:

$$C(s) + H_2O(g) \longrightarrow CO(g) + H_2(g)$$

- 1 mole of carbon reacts with 1 mole of water to form 1 mole of carbon monoxide and 1 mole of hydrogen.

- The carbon already exists as atoms so there are no C–C bonds to be broken. The energy needed to break the two bonds in the water (H–O bonds) is:

$$2 \times 463 = 926\,\text{kJ/mole}$$

- The energy released in the formation of carbon monoxide and hydrogen is $-358\,\text{kJ/mole}$ for the C–O bond and $-436\,\text{kJ/mole}$ for the H–H bond, making a total of $-794\,\text{kJ/mole}$.

- To find the net energy transfer for the reaction we combine the amount of energy taken in to break the bonds and the amount of energy released in bond formation:

$$926 + (-794) = +132\,\text{kJ/mole}$$

or $\Delta H = +132\,\text{kJ/mole}$

The positive number shows that less energy was released in bond formation than was needed to break existing bonds, telling us that the reaction is **endothermic**.

Bond energy calculations like this always follow the same pattern. You use this method to find the net energy transfer in reactions if an energy transfer diagram is not available.

? Questions

1 **a** What is meant by the term 'bond energy'?

   b What is the difference between the bond energy for making and breaking bonds and how do we indicate this difference?

2 Write balanced equations and then work out the net energy transfer for the following reactions:

   a   hydrogen   + bromine   ⟶   hydrogen bromide

   b   carbon   + hydrogen   ⟶   methane

   c carbon monoxide   + oxygen   ⟶   carbon dioxide

   d   nitrogen   + hydrogen   ⟶   ammonia.

0–m Key Ideas

- During a chemical reaction, energy must be supplied to break bonds and is released when bonds are formed.

- The net energy transfer in reactions can be calculated using known bond energies.

Reversible reactions

In some chemical reactions, the products formed immediately react together to produce the original reactants. This is what is known as a **reversible reaction**. Because a reversible reaction can go in both directions, when it is written down it is represented by a special double arrow with one half going in the forwards direction and the other backwards, like this:

A + B $\rightleftharpoons$ C + D
reactants   products

Examples of reversible reactions

When solid ammonium chloride is heated it decomposes into ammonia and hydrogen chloride (thermal decomposition). When these gases cool down they react and recombine to form ammonium chloride again:

ammonium chloride $\rightleftharpoons$ ammonia + hydrogen chloride
$NH_4Cl(s)$ $NH_3(g) + HCl(g)$
(white solid)   (colourless gases)

Another example of a reversible thermal decomposition is the reaction of hydrated copper sulphate with heat. When the familiar blue crystals of hydrated copper(II) sulphate are heated, the water is driven out of the crystals and evaporates, leaving white anhydrous copper(II) sulphate (hydrated means 'with water' and anhydrous means 'without water'):

hydrated copper(II) sulphate $\rightleftharpoons$ anhydrous copper(II) sulphate + water
$CuSO_4.xH_2O$ $\rightleftharpoons$ $CuSO_4$ + xH_2O
(blue)   (white)

If a few drops of water are then added to the white anhydrous copper(II) sulphate, the blue colour of the hydrated compound immediately returns. This reaction can be used as a laboratory test for water.

Yet another good example of a reversible reaction is the one between iodine monochloride (ICl) and chlorine gas. Iodine monochloride is a brown liquid, while chlorine is a green gas. They react together to form yellow crystals of iodine trichloride (ICl_3). In an atmosphere containing plenty of chlorine gas, iodine trichloride will be made and remain stable. If the concentration of chlorine falls then the iodine trichloride decomposes back to iodine monochloride and chlorine:

iodine monochloride + chlorine $\rightleftharpoons$ iodine trichloride
$ICl(l)$ + $Cl_2(g)$ $\rightleftharpoons$ $ICl_3(s)$
(brown)   (green)   (yellow)

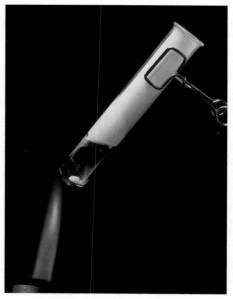

↑ **Figure 1:** The decomposition of ammonium chloride is a typical reversible reaction because the reaction goes in both directions very easily.

→ **Figure 2:** Iodine trichloride crystals decompose to give the iodine monochloride and chlorine gas from which it was formed.

Energy transfers in reversible reactions

If a reversible reaction is exothermic in one direction it will be endothermic in the other. The same amount of energy will be transferred in both cases. For example, hydrated copper sulphate needs energy supplied in the form of heat to give anhydrous copper sulphate and water. When water is added to anhydrous copper sulphate, energy in the form of heat is produced.

Equilibrium in reversible reactions

When a reversible reaction takes place in a closed system – one in which nothing can get in or out – then a state of equilibrium between the reactants and the products will be reached when the reaction occurs at exactly the same rate in each direction. Once this equilibrium is reached then the proportion of products and reactants in the mixture will stay the same. This situation is known as a **dynamic equilibrium**. The reactions are still going on – it is simply that the forward reaction is making products at exactly the same rate as the backward reaction is converting products back to reactants.

However, by changing the reaction conditions it is possible to change the position of the equilibrium – which changes the relative proportions of the reactants and products in the mixture. This is very important, because if we want to collect the products of a reaction we need as much product as possible in the reacting mixture.

Key Ideas

- In reversible reactions the products of the reaction can react to produce the original reactants.

- If a reversible reaction is exothermic in one direction it will be endothermic in the opposite direction. The same amount of energy is transferred in each case.

 - When a reversible reaction takes place in a closed system an equilibrium is reached where the reaction takes place at exactly the same rate in each direction.

Questions

1 What does the sign ⇌ mean when it is used in a reaction?

2 What is the main difference between a reversible reaction and an ordinary reaction? (Compare the reaction between iodine monochloride and chlorine with the reaction between hydrogen and chlorine to help with your explanation.)

3 In a reversible reaction, if the reaction in one direction is exothermic, the reaction in the opposite direction will be endothermic. Using ideas of energy and chemical bonds, explain why the *amount* of energy transferred is always exactly the same in the forward and reverse directions.

 4 a What is meant by a closed system?

   b In a closed system reversible reactions reach a dynamic equilibrium. What does this mean?

In a reversible reaction, the equilibrium position determines the relative amounts of reactants and products that will be present in the reacting mixture. For each reaction the equilibrium position depends very strongly on the conditions of temperature and pressure under which the reaction is taking place. It was a French chemist, Henri Le Chatelier, who first realised that by changing the reacting conditions (in particular the temperature and pressure) we can change the equilibrium position to give more product and less reactants in the final mixture. If we can shift the equilibrium position to the right, we will increase the yield of products (the proportion of products to reactants). This ability to manipulate the balance of reactants and products is very important when we look at industrial processes.

Moving the equilibrium – the rules

If a reaction is endothermic:

⊙ an increase in temperature supplies extra energy and so the yield of the products increases

⊙ a decrease in temperature decreases the yield of products.

If a reaction is exothermic:

⊙ a decrease in temperature increases the product yield

⊙ an increase in temperature decreases the product yield.

So in a reversible reaction we can alter the temperature to change the yield of chemicals in the equilibrium mixture.

But temperature is not the only important factor. Many reactions involving gases have a greater volume on one side of the reaction than the other. If we **raise** the pressure it encourages the reaction which produces less volume, while if we **lower** the pressure it encourages the reaction which produces more volume. So by choosing the appropriate pressure for our reaction we can increase the proportion of product in our final mixture.

The easiest way to understand these principles is to look at a real-life example. A typical case is that of the Haber process (see Section 4.8).

Equilibrium and the Haber process

The Haber process involves the reversible reaction between nitrogen and hydrogen to form ammonia:

$$N_2(g) + 3H_2(g) \rightleftharpoons 2NH_3(g)$$

ΔH is negative, so the forward reaction is exothermic

↓ Figure 2: The Haber process is remarkably efficient, because whatever the proportions of chemicals in the final reaction mixture, any unreacted nitrogen and hydrogen can be recycled and used again.

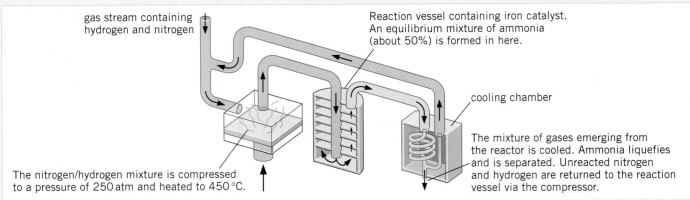

gas stream containing hydrogen and nitrogen

Reaction vessel containing iron catalyst. An equilibrium mixture of ammonia (about 50%) is formed in here.

cooling chamber

The nitrogen/hydrogen mixture is compressed to a pressure of 250 atm and heated to 450 °C.

The mixture of gases emerging from the reactor is cooled. Ammonia liquefies and is separated. Unreacted nitrogen and hydrogen are returned to the reaction vessel via the compressor.

On the left side of the equation there are 4 moles of gas (N_2 + $3H_2$). On the right side there are only 2 moles of gas ($2NH_3$). (As 1 mole of gas always takes up 22.4 litres at 0° C and atmospheric pressure, the volume is directly related to the number of moles.) So the